Stop Worrying
& Start Living

365 DAILY REFLECTIONS

Stop Worrying & Start Living

GARY ZIMAK

BEACON

Unless otherwise noted, Scripture passages have been taken from
the Revised Standard Version, Catholic Edition. Copyright 1946, 1952, 1971
by the Division of Christian Education of the National Council of Churches
of Christ in the USA. Used by permission. All rights reserved.

Quotes are taken from the English translation of the *Catechism of the Catholic
Church* for the United States of America (indicated as *CCC*), 2nd ed. Copyright
1997 by United States Catholic Conference—Libreria Editrice Vaticana.

ISBN: 978-1-942611-65-3 (hardcover)
ISBN: 978-1-942611-66-0 (softcover)

Cover design: Connie Gabbert
Interior: Finer Points Productions

Library of Congress Cataloging-in-Publication Data
Names: Zimak, Gary, author.
Title: Stop worrying and start living : 365 reflections / Gary Zimak.
Description: New, Expanded Third Edition. | North Palm Beach : Beacon
Publishing, 2016. | Includes bibliographical references and index.
Identifiers: LCCN 2016027346| ISBN 9781942611653 (hardcover : alk. paper) |
ISBN 9781942611660 (softcover : alk. paper) |
ISBN 9781942611677 (ebook : alk. paper)
Subjects: LCSH: Worry—Religious aspects—Catholic Church. | Devotional
calendars—Catholic Church. | Catholic Church—Doctrines.
Classification: LCC BV4908.5 .Z567 2016 |
DDC 242/.4—dc23

[1]

Printed in the United States of America

INTRODUCTION

God doesn't want you to worry, and he says so many times in the pages of the Bible. He also doesn't expect you to stop worrying all by yourself. He wants to help you and is willing to hold your hand and walk with you each day if you'll let him.

As someone who has struggled with anxiety for many years, I know just how painful it can be. After years of panic attacks, digestive problems, heart palpitations, and sleepless nights, I have discovered that a personal relationship with Jesus Christ can keep my worrying under control and allow me to experience peace. If it works for me, it can work for you.

In the following pages, you'll be able to hear God speak to you each day. Along with a short Bible verse (his inspired words), I have included a meditation that will assist you in living in his presence. Although the daily reading will only take a few minutes of your time, I encourage you to continue to meditate on it as you go about your daily routines. I'm confident that doing so will bring you a greater sense of peace. How can I be so sure? Not because I know you and your abilities. I don't. But I do know Jesus, and I know what happens when someone enters more deeply into a relationship with him. Reading his words in the Bible, speaking to him in prayer, spending time in his presence, and receiving the sacraments will change your life. You'll discover for yourself why he is called the Prince of Peace!

Now may the Lord of peace himself give you peace at all times in all ways. (2 Thessalonians 3:16)

(NOTE: Anxiety often has a biological component and sometimes must be treated with therapy and/or medication. Jesus can heal in many ways. If the verses and meditations contained in this book do not bring about a decrease in your anxiety, I strongly urge you to seek professional help. In certain cases, it may be necessary.)

JANUARY 1

And Mary said, "Behold, I am the
handmaid of the Lord; let it be to me
according to your word." (Luke 1:38)

Every day you and I have the opportunity to say yes to God. On the other hand we are also able to say no. Sometimes we forget that the Blessed Mother had free will and could have rejected Gabriel's invitation to become the mother of the Messiah. Mary wasn't given all the answers up front. She was told what God wanted her to know and that was it. Because of her great trust and her desire to do God's will, however, she consented to the request. As a result of her obedience, we received our Savior, who opened the gates of heaven for us.

Are you dealing with uncertainty right now? Is it hard to imagine why particular things are happening in your life? Mary understands. Ask her to help you trust in God's plan for your life and for the grace to say yes to whatever he sends your way.

*Mary, please help me to accept whatever
happens in my life, and grant me the grace
to say yes to God, even when I'm frightened.*

JANUARY 2

Come now, let us reason together, says the Lord.
Though your sins are like scarlet, they shall be as
white as snow; though they are red like crimson,
they shall become like wool. (Isaiah 1:18)

One of the greatest sources of anxiety is the overwhelming guilt caused by sin. Fortunately God's words to the prophet Isaiah remind us that there is no need to despair. Jesus is waiting to meet us in the sacrament of reconciliation.

Are you tired of carrying around the guilt of many sins? There is an answer. Take advantage of this great outpouring of God's mercy and make the decision to confess your sins, no matter how overwhelming they may be. You will not only feel peace, but you'll get to experience God's love and mercy firsthand!

God, I'm sorry for the times I have turned my
back on you. I long for the peace of knowing that
I'm doing your will. I look forward to meeting
you in this great sacrament of healing.

JANUARY 3

*Make a joyful noise to the Lord,
all the lands! (Psalm 100:1)*

How joyful are you today? No matter how bleak your life looks or what problems you are facing, God has given you another day—and he has big plans for you. He loves you unconditionally; nothing you do will ever change that. Everything that will happen to you today is sent by God as an expression of his love and designed to help you get to heaven. Finally, you have been created by God because he wants to share his joy with you. Feeling better?

While it's easy to forget facts like these when we're bombarded with the problems and challenges of daily life, it's important that we spend some time thinking about the many blessings we have received from God. The problems of this life are temporary, but the kingdom of heaven lasts forever. Rejoice and be glad!

*Thank you for blessing me in so many ways,
God. Help me to be more grateful!*

JANUARY 4

Jesus Christ is the same yesterday and today and for ever. (Hebrews 13:8)

Do you ever get frustrated with your life and wish you had lived during the time when Jesus walked the face of the earth? If you were sick or in need, you could have simply approached him and asked for a healing. If your faith grew weak, it would have been strengthened by witnessing one of his numerous miracles. It's hard to imagine the security we would feel just by being in his presence.

Jesus Christ is still with us; he has not changed. He continues to speak to us, and we can speak with him. We can visit him at our local adoration chapel and receive him in the Eucharist at Mass. He still can (and does) perform miracles if we give him a chance. Don't make the mistake of treating Christ as a historical figure. Speak with him daily and get to know him. He is the best friend you'll ever have.

*Help me to remember that you
are always with me, Jesus, and allow
me to see you through the eyes of faith.*

JANUARY 5

"Let not your hearts be troubled; believe
in God, believe also in me." (John 14:1)

Even though we have done nothing to deserve it, Jesus
promises that there is a place in heaven reserved for us. Once
this temporary life is over, we will be given the opportunity
to live with him forever in paradise. It will be a life without
sickness, financial problems, or worries of any kind. Best of
all, it will last forever.

So why do we allow our hearts to be troubled? Typically
it's because we lose sight of the big picture. While it's no secret that we will experience problems during our time on
earth, none of our problems will last forever. They will either
disappear in this life or come to an end when we die. On the
other hand, the happiness of heaven will last forever. Spend
some time thinking about Christ's words today. I bet your
heart will feel a little less troubled.

*Lord, help me to stay focused on the fact that
I was created to live with you in heaven.
May I never forget your words of comfort, especially
when my problems begin to overwhelm me.*

JANUARY 6

In the beginning God created the
heavens and the earth. (Genesis 1:1)

Have you ever dealt with a problem so serious that you didn't think it was fixable? As you explore potential solutions in your head, you become increasingly hopeless and conclude that nothing will turn things around. Sound familiar?

Sometimes we forget just how powerful God is. We spend so much time dwelling on the mountain standing before us that we lose sight of the fact that God is infinitely bigger than the mountain. If he created the heavens and the earth, he can certainly fix any problem you are facing. And while he may take his time or answer your prayer in a way that displeases you, it's not because he doesn't care or because he's weak. It's because he loves you and knows what's best. God is all-powerful—he can do anything. Always keep that in mind when you pray.

Help me to remember that you are
greater than my problems, God, and
allow my trust in you to increase.

JANUARY 7

"Behold, I stand at the door and knock;
if any one hears my voice and opens the
door, I will come in to him and eat with
him, and he with me." (Revelation 3:20)

It never ceases to amaze me how Jesus will not force his way into our lives. As someone who ignored him for many years, I can personally vouch for that fact. What he will do, however, is knock, and knock, and knock again. Once we finally open the door and let him in, we experience peace like we've never felt before.

Are you anxious about something or someone in your life? Jesus is knocking on your door. You can choose to worry (which is useless), or you can choose to open the door and invite him into your life. He will not only help you with your problems, but he will share with you the gift of his peace. The choice is yours.

*Today I will open the door and invite you
into my life, Jesus. Allow me to feel the
supernatural peace that only you can give.*

JANUARY 8

"And which of you by being anxious can add one cubit to his span of life?" (Matthew 6:27)

Jesus is very clear when he reminds us that worrying is not a productive activity. Giving way to anxiety cannot help us at all. So why do we worry? Many times we do it because it's become a habit or we've lost sight of God's providence.

Worrying certainly isn't a good use of our time, but don't be fooled into thinking that it doesn't produce results. It does. Unfortunately, those results are not good for you. While none of your problems have killed you yet (thanks be to God!), excessive worrying can. At the very least, it can make you physically or emotionally ill. Let's turn to the Jesus today and ask him to help us stop worrying.

Jesus, I know that worrying serves no useful purpose, but I am too weak to stop. Please help me to trust in you more and to worry less.

JANUARY 9

Are you tired of waiting for God to answer your prayers? Do you sometimes feel that he doesn't even hear you? The prophet Micah provides us with some wise advice and reminds us that God does indeed hear us . . . we just need to give him some time.

We live in a fast-paced world, and we have a tendency to be impatient. If we send a text message or an e-mail and don't receive an immediate reply, we get frustrated and wonder if we're being heard. That same kind of impatience often spills over into our prayer life as well.

Rest assured that God always hears your prayers. His timing is perfect and he will respond when the time is right. Don't rush him!

*Dear Jesus, I struggle with impatience, and sometimes
I get frustrated with your apparent lack of response
to my prayers. Please increase my trust in you and
help me to wait patiently for your response.*

JANUARY 10

The King of Israel, the Lord, is in your midst;
you shall fear evil no more. (Zephaniah 3:15)

The world can be a scary place. We are surrounded with temptation and we sometimes feel too weak to fight against the power of Satan.

Here's some good news: The devil can't force you to do anything. He can lie to you, he can pressure you, he can tempt you with all kinds of thoughts and desires, but he can't make you sin. On the other hand, the power of almighty God is infinite. As long as you lean on him, you can overcome any temptation that you encounter. Best of all, you don't have to worry about him not being available. The God of heaven and earth is right in your midst and ready to help you!

Thank you for your constant presence in my life,
God. Please keep me from falling into sin today.

JANUARY 11

For the sake of Christ, then, I am content with
weaknesses, insults, hardships, persecutions,
and calamities; for when I am weak, then
I am strong. (2 Corinthians 12:10)

I have always considered myself to be a weak person. Through the years I have given up on many projects, done things I was ashamed of, and failed to do things I should have done. In addition I spent many years trying to overcome my excessive worrying.

In spite of my weakness, St. Paul's words to the people of Corinth give me a great deal of hope. He assures me that it's okay to be weak. More important, his statement reminds me just how much I need God in my life. On my own I can't avoid sin, stop worrying, or persevere in prayer. But with Christ's help, I can do all things!

May my weakness always remind me how much
I need you, Jesus. Help me to be strong today.

JANUARY 12

Then the Lord put forth his hand and touched my mouth; and the Lord said to me, "Behold, I have put my words in your mouth." (Jeremiah 1:9)

Jeremiah didn't have a great deal of confidence, which at first glance would seem to be a big problem for a prophet. Proclaiming God's Word to people who don't want to hear it isn't exactly a job for wimps! Trying to convince God that he chose the wrong guy, Jeremiah insisted that he was too young and he wasn't a good speaker.

God knew better, however. He assured the reluctant prophet that he would be given the words to deliver to the people.

Too many times we fail to recognize that if God calls us to do something, he'll give us the help we need. Whether it's stepping out of our comfort zone to help others or simply accepting the suffering that comes our way, he will not desert us. As the old saying goes, "If God brings you to it, he will see you through it!"

God, I'm grateful that you will always provide me with the strength I need to carry out any task you give me.

JANUARY 13

O Lord my God, in you I take refuge; save me
from all my pursuers, and deliver me. (Psalm 7:1)

I am embarrassed to admit how many times I have faced
problems and failed to ask God for help. While it should be
the first thing we do, it's often the last. Why is that? Could it
be that we don't trust him? Is it because most of the problems
we face are worldly in nature and we don't think that's
his area of expertise?

Whatever the reason, this is something we need to fix.
God loves us and wants to be intimately involved in our
lives. He is also bigger than any potential problem we could
ever face. Yesterday is gone and tomorrow is not guaranteed.
Let's live in the present moment and make today the day that
we start turning to him with all of our needs.

*As I begin this new day, Lord, I ask for your help with
all of my earthly problems and concerns. Thank you
for caring enough to want to get involved in my life.*

JANUARY 14

The Lord is good, a stronghold in the
day of trouble; he knows those who
take refuge in him. (Nahum 1:7)

I have a difficult time dealing with change and uncertainty.
Stability is something that brings me a great deal of comfort,
and I suspect that I'm not the only one who feels this way.
Dealing with change on a daily basis is a big source of anxiety for many of us.

Here's something to think about today: God never
changes. He is the same yesterday, today, and tomorrow. A
relationship with him provides us with a source of stability
in a very unstable world. He is not affected by the weather,
the stock market, or even our moods. He is always the same.
I like that!

*Thank you for being an unchanging
stronghold for me, God. I'm grateful
that I can take refuge in you today.*

JANUARY 15

But Peter said, "I have no silver and gold, but I give you what I have; in the name of Jesus Christ of Nazareth, rise and walk." (Acts 3:6)

There is no doubt that money is necessary. God understands that we all have bills to pay. But there is something more precious than monetary wealth. In this Bible verse Peter's response to the beggar teaches us a valuable lesson.

Initially it appears that the apostle was unable to help the man. In reality, however, he was able to help him in a big way. Even if we are living in poverty, you and I have the ability to turn to Jesus in prayer. It costs nothing and can produce incredible results. Never forget that your ability to pray is a greater treasure than all the riches in the world.

Dear Jesus, thank you for always hearing me when I speak to you. Help me to better appreciate the value of prayer.

JANUARY 16

Cast all your anxieties on him, for he
cares about you. (1 Peter 5:7)

Isn't it great to have a friend? When faced with a problem,
it's a blessing to have someone to turn to in your time of
need. Even if your friend can't fix the issue, it's comforting
to know that someone is there for you.

As wonderful as it can be to have a shoulder to cry on,
it's even better to have a friend who can help you solve your
problem. Jesus, the Lord of the universe, wants to be your
friend. He wants you to hand over all of your problems to
him. Why? Not only because he cares about you and doesn't
want you to worry, but because he knows the best way to
handle the difficulties in your life. Let's give him a chance.

Thank you for caring so much about me, Jesus.
I give you my anxieties and struggles. Please allow
me to experience your supernatural peace.

JANUARY 17

And Moses said to the people, "Fear not, stand firm, and see the salvation of the Lord, which he will work for you today; for the Egyptians whom you see today, you shall never see again." (Exodus 14:13)

"Trust me."

Depending on who is speaking, this is arguably one of the most challenging phrases in the English language. Suppose you meet a complete stranger on the street and he asks to borrow a hundred dollars, promising to repay you in a week. Would you trust him? Chances are you wouldn't, and with good reason. How about if your spouse or a close friend asked you for the same loan? It would probably be much easier to trust.

Speaking through Moses, God the Father promised the Israelites that they would be delivered from slavery. He assured them that the Egyptians would no longer be a threat. What proof did he offer? None, other than the fact that he was God. Are you willing to trust almighty God with the problems that you are facing? You should—he has a really good record of delivering on his promises!

God, I know that you love me and
want what is best for me. Help me to
trust you with all of my problems.

JANUARY 18

And I will walk among you, and
will be your God, and you shall be
my people. (Leviticus 26:12)

I have always been impressed with business executives who are willing to roll up their sleeves, pitch in, and work side by side with their employees. I have seen this play out not only on television, but in real life as well. If done for the right reasons, it demonstrates a certain sense of humility and compassion.

When we stop and think about it, the idea of God walking among us is mind-boggling. But that's exactly what happened when the Word became flesh. While still retaining his divinity, Jesus Christ literally became one of us. What's even more astonishing is that he is still with us today. In the Eucharist Christ is fully present and can be encountered at Mass, in tabernacles, and in adoration chapels around the world.

It's wonderful to know we can visit him in person whenever we want. It definitely beats worrying!

Thank you for being so close to me,
Jesus. I can't wait to see you soon!

JANUARY 19

"Do not be afraid, my son, because we have become poor. You have great wealth if you fear God and refrain from every sin and do what is pleasing in his sight." (Tobit 4:21)

When I speak at parishes and conferences, I meet many people who are worried about money. In fact, financial anxiety is one of the biggest sources of stress in the world today.

Tobit's words to his son show great wisdom and indicate that he understands the true meaning of wealth. Having an abundance of money will make us happy only for a while. Furthermore, being rich can even hurt our chances of getting to heaven. No matter how little money you have, the only way you are truly poor is if you don't have a relationship with God. Even though it may not feel like it when you're struggling to pay your bills, if you have Jesus in your life, you are very wealthy!

God, I confess—all too often I get distracted by the things of the world. Thank you for your presence in my life; with you by my side, I am truly wealthy.

JANUARY 20

Blessed be the God and Father of our
Lord Jesus Christ, who has blessed us
in Christ with every spiritual blessing in
the heavenly places. (Ephesians 1:3)

Because we're human we sometimes take our blessings for granted. As an example, for many years I woke up every morning and never thanked God for giving me another day. Instead I complained that I was too tired, too hot, or too cold, or that I didn't feel like going to work. It took a frightening health scare to make me realize just how selfish and ungrateful I was.

In this excerpt from his letter to the Ephesians, St. Paul reminds us that in Christ we have received "every spiritual blessing" imaginable. Thinking about that can make us feel thankful even in the midst of great suffering. We are very blessed, my friends. Let's be full of joy and gratitude!

*Heavenly Father, thank you for blessing me
with the gift of your Son. Through him I have
been redeemed, and I am very grateful!*

JANUARY 21

And he said to them, "Why are you afraid,
O men of little faith?" Then he rose and
rebuked the winds and the sea; and there
was a great calm. (Matthew 8:26)

Before I got my driver's license, I took a driving class at my high school. One of the topics we were taught was how to handle skidding on ice. Because of this training I knew exactly what to do if I encountered this situation . . . or so I thought!

One day it happened for real, and I somehow forgot everything I had learned. After I slammed on the brakes and turned the steering wheel like a madman, my car proceeded to spin in circles until safely coming to a stop.

The apostles knew that Jesus could perform miracles, but they panicked when the storm kicked up. We often make the same mistake when unexpected problems arise in our lives. Jesus understands. Continue to turn to him and ask for help. While you're at it, ask him to strengthen your faith. Eventually you'll find it easier to trust him.

Jesus, thank you for putting up with
me when I begin to panic. Please
help me to trust you more.

JANUARY 22

"I beg you, my child, to look at the heaven and the earth and see everything that is in them, and recognize that God did not make them out of things that existed." (2 Maccabees 7:28)

Sometimes we have a tendency to look at our difficulties and consider them unfixable. If not controlled, this way of thinking can cause us to become hopeless and fall into despair.

With all due respect to those who suffer, there is no such thing as a hopeless situation. Although it may not seem like it at times, every problem can be solved. God is all-powerful and bigger than any issue we could ever face. Need proof? He created the entire universe out of nothing. That's what I call powerful! Have faith in his abilities and ask him to fix the problems in your life. Be persistent, patient, and willing to accept his answer.

Almighty Father, you created everything out of nothing. Please take my problems and handle them using your infinite wisdom and power.

JANUARY 23

Holy, holy, holy is the Lord of hosts; the whole earth is full of his glory. (Isaiah 6:3)

Are you able to see God in everyone you meet, everywhere you go, and everything that happens to you? It can be a challenge to do so, especially with all the distractions we encounter every day. In order to be peaceful, however, we need to come up with a way to constantly live in the presence of God.

Although it doesn't come naturally to me, I have learned to be thankful for the many blessings in my life: each new day, the warmth of the sun, the gift of rainfall, the intricacy of the human body, and the gift of Jesus' real presence in the Eucharist. By acknowledging God's gifts to us each day, we gradually begin to realize that he truly is present in our lives. You might have to work at it in the beginning, but it will gradually become easier. Give it a try, and soon you'll begin to see God everywhere!

> *Thank you for filling the earth with your glory,*
> *God. Strengthen my inner eyesight so I can see*
> *you more clearly in the ordinary events of life.*

JANUARY 24

Trust in the Lord with all your heart, and do not rely on your own insight. (Proverbs 3:5)

Even though God has proven his trustworthiness many times over the years (in salvation history and in our lives), trusting in him "with all your heart" is not an easy thing to do. Do you ever wish that God would give you the details of what lies ahead in your life? We would be so much more peaceful if we knew what was coming . . . or would we?

Surprisingly, uncertainty can draw us closer to God. Because we don't know what lies ahead, we have the opportunity to trust in his providence. If you find it difficult to trust, ask God to help you. Over time you'll see the benefit of trusting your future to your heavenly Father, who loves you more than you could ever imagine.

Even though I think I know what's best for me,
Father, I understand that you know better.
I long to trust you with all my heart.

JANUARY 25

*For in everything, O Lord, you have exalted
and glorified your people; and you have
not neglected to help them at all times
and in all places. (Wisdom 19:22)*

One of the benefits of reading the Bible is that it helps us to understand just how much God has helped his people through the years. Despite the fact that the Israelites disobeyed him many times, he never deserted them. Looking back over my years as a lukewarm Catholic, I can see a similar story. God never gave up on me and was always there to bail me out.

When moving forward, it's sometimes helpful to look back. I can think of many "hopeless" situations that worked out much better than I could have ever imagined. Even though I don't know what will happen to me tomorrow, I know that God has always been there for me in the past. If he didn't desert me then, why would he abandon me now?

*Thank you for your constant love and protection,
dear God. I can face the future with confidence,
knowing that you will always be there with me.*

JANUARY 26

"And I tell you, Ask and it will be given you; seek, and you will find; knock, and it will be opened to you." (Luke 11:9)

While this is one of Jesus' best-known messages, it's also one of the most misunderstood. We all know what it's like not to receive something we asked for in prayer. What gives? Didn't Jesus say that if we ask, we'll receive?

Yes, he did, but he never said *what* we will receive! In the often-ignored verses that follow this statement (see Luke 11:11–13), Jesus explains that our heavenly Father will never give us anything harmful. Why? Because he loves us too much! Even though we think we know what we need, we often don't. Many of the things that appear good to us can get in the way of our relationship with God. If he says no, take comfort in the fact that it's his way of saying, "I love you."

Although it's not easy for me to hear an answer of "no," Jesus, I understand that it's necessary. Thank you for loving me too much to give me anything that would harm me.

JANUARY 27

He who has the Son has life; he who has not
the Son of God has not life. (1 John 5:12)

Eternity is a difficult concept to grasp. Since everything in this life comes to an end, it's not easy to understand the idea of forever. On the other hand, we all know what it's like to enjoy something so much that we don't want it to end.

While many things in this world can bring us happiness, nothing can come close to the gift given to us by Jesus Christ. He gave his very life so that you and I could live in his Father's kingdom forever. Even though we can't fully comprehend it, we should be grateful and rejoice. We will never receive a greater gift.

Thank you, Jesus, for making it possible
for me to live forever in heaven.

JANUARY 28

And the Lord came and stood forth, calling as at other times, "Samuel! Samuel!" And Samuel said, "Speak, for your servant hears." (1 Samuel 3:10)

I have great news for you. God wants to speak to you today. I don't know what he wants to tell you, but I know with certainty that he has a personal message for you. How can you hear what he has to say? By listening!

Samuel teaches us a great lesson with his openness to hearing God's voice. Most of us have no problem approaching him when we need something, yet we're not as willing to ask how we can serve him. Instead of "Speak, for your servant hears," we often say, "Listen, for your servant is speaking!"

God has something to say to you today. He wants to speak to you in prayer, through the pages of the Bible, through nature, and even through other people. The only way you're going to hear his message, however, is by listening!

God, I'm listening for your voice today.

JANUARY 29

For we brought nothing into the
world, and we cannot take anything
out of the world. (1 Timothy 6:7)

I have always been a collector. Over the years I have collected many different items: comic books, baseball cards, records, newspapers, magazines, and much more. As a result, I've accumulated lots of "stuff."

Eventually I began to question my actions. I spent a great deal of time and money collecting items that were hidden in closets and under beds. What was the point? I rarely looked at my prized collectibles. Furthermore, I was concerned that these fragile items would deteriorate over the years and I would no longer have them.

When we die we won't be bringing anything with us. All we'll have is the fruit of our good works. Why is it that accumulating and holding on to our possessions takes up so much time and causes us so much stress?

*On this day, God, I ask that you take away my
desire to accumulate excessive material goods and
replace it with a desire for spiritual treasures.*

JANUARY 30

And after a while the brook dried up, because there was no rain in the land. (1 Kings 17:7)

One of the ways that God speaks to us is through the circumstances of ordinary life. Sometimes what seems to be a disaster ends up being a great blessing. My career as a full-time speaker and author resulted from a job layoff, and my friendship with Jesus Christ blossomed because of a health crisis.

Before you write off an event as a coincidence or bad luck, read about what happened to the prophet Elijah (see 1 Kings 17:1–16). God caused Elijah's water supply to dry up because he wanted the prophet to move on to Zarephath. Could God be calling you to do something?

Pay attention to what is happening around you. There's a good chance that God is speaking to you without using words.

Jesus, today I will listen for your voice
in the daily events of my life.

JANUARY 31

Is any one among you suffering? Let him pray. Is any cheerful? Let him sing praise (James 5:13)

For most people of faith, it's not difficult to pray when suffering. In fact, it's a great blessing to be able to do so. Even when I was an extremely lukewarm Catholic, I didn't have to be reminded to pray when I was facing a crisis. As the old saying goes, "There are no atheists in foxholes."

On the other hand, it's not quite as intuitive to pray when things are going well. We have a tendency to forget that God is responsible for the good times as well as the bad. What are you thankful for today? The gift of a new day? His unconditional love? Family and friends? Whatever it is, be thankful for it because God made it happen!

You have blessed me in so many ways,
God. Thank you for everything!

FEBRUARY 1

"Is anything too hard for the Lord?"
(Genesis 18:14)

Good question, isn't it? Now before you answer with a resounding no, let's think about it for a minute. How many times have you failed to pray for an "impossible" situation because you thought it would be useless? How about those times when impatience caused you to stop praying because you assumed that God wasn't listening? Even though we all know that nothing is too hard for him, we constantly forget it.

It doesn't matter what type of crisis you're facing; God can fix it. Not only can he cure cancer, mend the most broken relationship, or allow you to find a job after several years of unemployment, but he can help you to stick with your prayer life, give you the grace to overcome your "favorite" sin, or enable you to stop worrying. Nothing, and I mean nothing, is too hard for our God!

*When things seem overwhelming to
me, remind me that nothing is too hard
for you, God. You are amazing!*

FEBRUARY 2

And when the time came for their purification according to the law of Moses, they brought him up to Jerusalem to present him to the Lord. (Luke 2:22)

Today we celebrate the day when Jesus was officially presented in the Temple. Sometimes referred to as "Candlemas," this feast commemorates the first public appearance of the Light of the World.

If you have ever tried to walk across a dark room, you know just how treacherous it can be. In the darkness, that pair of shoes or pile of books can cause you to take an unexpected and painful tumble. In a similar way, the world in which we live can be a dark place. The obstacles that we face, however, are much more dangerous than random items on the floor. Fortunately there is no need to be afraid. That same Light of the World who was brought to the Temple two thousand years ago is still beside us today. And his light shines brighter than any night-light.

Jesus, help me to navigate the dark road of life by acting as my light. With you by my side, I am not afraid of any temptation.

FEBRUARY 3

It is for discipline that you have to endure. God is treating you as sons; for what son is there whom his father does not discipline? (Hebrews 12:7)

In my youth I spent many hours in my room—and it wasn't always voluntary. When I acted inappropriately my parents would send me to my room as a punishment. As you might expect, I hated it. When I look back now, however, it was a valuable learning experience, and I'm glad my parents did what they did. Parental discipline is a sign of love. My parents didn't send me to my room because they felt like making me suffer. They did it because they were trying to teach me something. They knew that I would be in big trouble as an adult if I didn't learn to control my behavior, and they cared too much about me to let that happen.

Our heavenly Father loves us greatly, and he sometimes expresses that love through discipline. What we view as "bad luck" is actually that fatherly discipline playing out in our lives. If you are going through a hard time, ask God what he is trying to teach you. It might require some persistence on your part, but it will eventually become clear.

Father, as I look at the difficulties I face this day, show me what you're trying to teach me through them.

FEBRUARY 4

O Lord, my heart is not lifted up, my eyes are not raised too high; I do not occupy myself with things too great and too marvelous for me. (Psalm 131:1)

No matter how hard we try, sometimes we just can't figure out why God allows certain things to happen. The events of September 11, 2001, provide us with an unforgettable example. Out-of-control forest fires, floods and hurricanes, and senseless school shootings are other poignant examples.

I have spent many unproductive hours trying to understand why God didn't let me get that job, why a potential girlfriend rejected me, or why a "can't-miss" business idea failed miserably. Sometimes I can see that it worked out for the best. In other cases it's not so obvious.

God wants us to trust him, and that requires accepting the fact that we won't always be able to figure out his reasoning. While the uncertainty can sometimes cause us anxiety, it can also bring us great comfort if we stop fighting and give him the benefit of the doubt.

God, thank you for the gift of uncertainty
and for showing me what an opportunity
it is to trust in your providence.

FEBRUARY 5

"So you have sorrow now, but I will see you again and your hearts will rejoice, and no one will take your joy from you." (John 16:22)

It's always easier to endure suffering when we know it's temporary. I don't enjoy sitting in traffic, but I can handle it because I know there's an end in sight. The same applies to being sick with a cold or dealing with inclement weather. Keeping my focus on the fact that better days are ahead can lift my spirits in a hurry.

Jesus understands that we all have problems in this life. He knows we will face some degree of suffering each day. No matter how painful it may be, however, earthly suffering is temporary, and that's what God wants us to remember. Why not take advantage of your suffering and offer it up while you still have it? By doing so you can help yourself and others get to heaven, a place where there will be eternal happiness.

Jesus, in my better moments I know that the suffering in my life is not permanent. Increase my desire to offer it up for the salvation of souls.

FEBRUARY 6

If you have many possessions, make your gift from them in proportion; if few, do not be afraid to give according to the little you have. (Tobit 4:8)

Fear of poverty causes many of us to spend sleepless nights worrying about job layoffs and stock market crashes. If we're not careful, this anxiety can cause us to hoard our money just in case we need it.

Although it can be difficult, God wants us to trust him and share what we have with those in need. Does this mean we should donate our rent or food money to charity? No! That would be irresponsible. What it does mean is that we should prayerfully consider how much money we *truly* need for a rainy day. There are people who could use some of that "what-if" money to put food on their table. Even though it might not seem like it, this kind of bold generosity will bring us great peace.

Jesus, today I will trust more in you and less in my material wealth. Grant me the grace to be willing to share whatever I have with those in need.

FEBRUARY 7

"Blessed are they who hunger and thirst for righteousness, for they shall be satisfied." (Matthew 5:6)

How often do you pray for spiritual favors? While it's true that we all need material things in order to survive in the world, these items are temporary and will either decay or remain behind when we die. Spiritual gifts, on the other hand, will help us get to heaven.

In the Sermon on the Mount, Jesus assures us that our hunger and thirst for righteousness will be satisfied without exception. How badly do you want to overcome your anger, pride, selfishness, and impatience? Do you really want to be able to trust more and worry less? If so, when was the last time you asked God to help you?

The fact that you want to break away from your bad habits and become holy is a good thing. Now it's time to take it to the next level by asking Jesus for help. You can rest assured that he won't ignore your plea!

I want to grow closer to you, Jesus. I know I can't do it on my own, but with your grace I can overcome what hinders me and holds me back from growing spiritually.

FEBRUARY 8

Set your minds on things that are above, not on things that are on earth. (Colossians 3.2)

Rainy days tend to bring me down. But rather than just accepting that I'm going to be miserable every time it rains, I have learned to look at the positive aspects of rain: It provides drinking water, it allows the plants to grow, it helps the farmers, and so on. If I focus on the fact that rain is a gift from God, I find I can be happy even when it rains.

Each of us faces difficulties on a daily basis. Dwelling on them too much makes us unhappy. On the other hand, trying to see God in every situation lifts our spirits and helps us to maintain a positive outlook. Furthermore, all of the problems that we face in this life are temporary. There is a light at the end of the tunnel!

When I'm tempted to struggle with my problems today, God, instead I will keep my focus on you and the rewards of heaven.

FEBRUARY 9

And he said, "Naked I came from my mother's womb, and naked shall I return; the Lord gave, and the Lord has taken away; blessed be the name of the Lord." (Job 1:21)

Can you imagine tragically losing your property and your children and saying the above words? As incomprehensible as it may seem, that's exactly what Job did. Why in the world would he bless the name of the Lord after a tragedy like this?

Job's words indicate that he understood that everything and everyone in his life was on loan to him from God. He was also well aware of the fact that all that happened in his life, good and bad, was an expression of God's providence. If you have trouble feeling the same way, don't panic. Most of us aren't in Job's league when it comes to accepting misfortune. What we can (and should) do is pray for the grace to trust God as he did. That grace will give us great peace.

Thank you for caring for me, Father.
Help me to see everything that happens
to me as an expression of your love.

FEBRUARY 10

Now hope that is seen is not hope. For who
hopes for what he sees? (Romans 8:24)

Seeing is believing! We've all heard this expression many times. Putting it into practice, however, can definitely hurt our relationship with Jesus. It can also make us miserable.

Throughout history God has promised many things. And while many of his promises were fulfilled in the pages of the Bible, there are still uncertainties in our own lives. Will heaven really be as good as he promises? Can a sinner like me really make it there? Will all of the crises in my life really work out for the best?

Like it or not, we are not going to have all the answers in this life. Fortunately we receive the virtue of hope when we are baptized. That special gift helps us to believe that heaven exists, that it will be great, and that we can get there. Sometimes believing involves a lot more than just seeing!

*Jesus, please increase my hope so I can
believe more deeply in your promises.*

FEBRUARY 11

When God saw what they did, how they turned away from their evil way, God repented of the evil which he had said he would do to them; and he did not do it. (Jonah 3:10)

There will always be times when we'd rather do what we want and not what God wants. Jonah is a great example of someone who wanted to do things his way. After reluctantly going to Ninevah (after a layover in the belly of a large fish), Jonah proclaimed God's message of repentance, and the people responded. Even though Jonah didn't want to be there and didn't feel that the Ninevites deserved a second chance, God worked through him and got the job done.

What's the moral of the story? If you don't feel like praying, pray anyway. If you don't feel like reaching out to a friend, do it anyway. If you feel like giving up, keep going. Don't base your spiritual life on feelings. God can work through you in amazing ways, even if you don't feel a thing!

God, I don't want to get in your way today. Please use me to do your work, even when I don't feel like it.

FEBRUARY 12

I want you to be free from anxieties.

(1 Corinthians 7:32)

I often open my parish talks with these words. Even though they were written by St. Paul, this message was inspired by God. Therefore we now can be sure that God wants us to be free from anxiety. How does that make you feel?

For those of us who have a tendency to worry, these words can be frightening. After all, we don't want to offend God by worrying when we're not supposed to. Don't let it frighten you, because this is great news! If God wants us to be free from anxieties, then it must be possible. How can a chronic worrier learn to break free from anxiety, you ask? The secret is to let God help you. No matter what you might be facing, you can ask him to help you stop worrying. Make it a point to ask him today, and watch what happens.

I know you don't want me to worry, Jesus!
When I trust in you, my anxieties melt
away. Please help me to trust you more!

FEBRUARY 13

With him who fears the Lord it will go
well at the end; on the day of his death
he will be blessed. (Sirach 1:13)

What's this? A Bible verse endorsing fear? In a book designed
to help you overcome anxiety? Absolutely! I love this verse
because it reminds us that fear of the Lord is a good thing.

Although the terminology has fallen out of favor, true
fear of the Lord is rooted in love. Furthermore, it is a gift of
the Holy Spirit. In its purest form this gift helps us to love
God so much that we would never want to offend him by
committing a sin. In its most primitive form, it can help us
to avoid sin because we're afraid of the consequences. While
love of God should be the motivation for performing good
deeds, we're human and sometimes act out of selfishness.
Avoiding sin is always a good thing, even if our motive is less
than perfect. At the end of our lives, this healthy kind of fear
will bear great fruit.

Jesus, I love you! Please grant me the
grace to avoid sinning today.

FEBRUARY 14

We walk by faith, not by sight.
(2 Corinthians 5:7)

I'm not going to kid you—the world can be a frightening place. A quick look at the TV news or the Internet reminds us that terrorism, severe weather, immorality, and financial volatility are real threats. When we throw our personal issues into the mix, it is very easy to become overwhelmed by fear.

Fortunately for us Jesus Christ is bigger than any of these threats. So why do we worry? Mainly because we do the exact opposite of what St. Paul states in his letter to the people of Corinth—we walk by *sight* and not by *faith*.

Even though God is greater than any problem you can ever face, you won't believe it until you encounter him daily. Make it a point today to spend some time in silence with Jesus. As your faith in him grows, you'll begin to see exactly what St. Paul means.

*Today I will focus more on you, God, and
less on the threats that surround me.*

FEBRUARY 15

"I will put enmity between you and the woman, and between your seed and her seed; he shall bruise your head, and you shall bruise his heel." (Genesis 3:15)

This verse, known as the Protoevangelium ("first Gospel"), is one of the most important messages contained in the Bible. Immediately after Adam and Eve sinned, God promised that a Messiah, born of a woman, would one day defeat Satan and the power of evil forever.

So how does this message help us when we're struggling to make it through the day? As good as it is, this promise isn't going to help us pay our bills or deal with a serious illness. Although we may not realize it, all of our hope lies in this message. You have been redeemed by Jesus Christ. As a result, it is possible to live forever in heaven. All your earthly problems are temporary and will disappear in a relatively short period of time. The happiness of heaven lasts forever. Thinking about that really helps keep things in perspective.

Father, deepen my appreciation for the gift of your Son, Jesus. Thank you for sending him to redeem me.

FEBRUARY 16

And he told them a parable, to the effect that they ought always to pray and not lose heart. (Luke 18:1)

Sometimes the Bible can be confusing. In fact, even St. Peter felt that it could be difficult to understand (see 2 Peter 3:16). Fortunately we have the guidance of the Church to help us grasp the meaning of God's message in Scripture.

On the other hand, the meaning of some verses is crystal clear. Before he presents Jesus' parable of the unjust judge, St. Luke gives us the main message of the story: We should not stop praying because God isn't answering quickly enough.

We've all been through this, and you may be going through it right now. God hears your prayers. Don't assume that his delayed response means that he's not listening. Keep praying. The Lord has a plan, and his timing is always perfect.

Even though you seem to be taking a long time to answer some of my prayers, God, I'll keep praying because I know you're listening.

FEBRUARY 17

Great peace have those who love your law;
nothing can make them stumble. (Psalm 119:165)

Looking for the secret to peace? Here it is! While this is not one of the more popular messages in the world today, it's the absolute truth. If we love God we will desire to obey his teachings as proclaimed through the Church. Doing so will bring us great peace.

This is such a simple and effective message, but it's one that is violated constantly. One of the reasons is our society's dislike of the word *law*. Whether it's God's law or man's law, people don't like to be told what to do. How can we get past this? We can start by getting to know Jesus Christ. We do this by speaking to him daily and reading the Gospels. Knowing him personally will lead to a greater desire to truly follow him by living out the teachings of the Church. Peace will then follow!

*Jesus, deepen my love for you and for
the teachings of your Church.*

FEBRUARY 18

He who observes the wind will not sow; and he who regards the clouds will not reap. (Ecclesiastes 11:4)

While there is nothing wrong with being cautious, we can take it too far. The fear of a bad outcome can lead to complete paralysis. As an anxious person by nature, I can come up with a negative spin on just about everything. Allowing myself to do that, however, would not be a good thing.

We don't know what will happen to us tomorrow or the day after. And while God wants us to exercise caution and avoid being reckless, he also wants us to trust him. Abraham, Moses, and the Blessed Mother didn't have all the answers, but they trusted in God's plan for their lives. Start by taking baby steps. If you feel that God is calling you to do something, pray about it and discuss it with trusted friends. If you still feel you should do it, then go for it. Even if you are dead wrong and it wasn't God's will, he can fix it!

I trust in your providence, God. Grant me the grace to avoid obsessing over negative outcomes.

FEBRUARY 19

"The time is fulfilled, and the kingdom of God is at hand; repent and believe in the gospel." (Mark 1:15)

Jesus is coming. Look busy!

Despite its funny intent, this popular bumper sticker message does contain an element of truth. One day we will have to account for our actions, so we'd better get to work!

In his first recorded words in St. Mark's Gospel, Jesus proclaims that the kingdom of God has arrived and it's time to get busy. While Christ's words imply a sense of urgency, there is also an element of comfort contained in them. Our Savior is here! He is with us, and following him will lead us to heaven. What's the catch? We must repent and turn away from our sins. And because our sins can cause great stress, following Jesus' command will bring us peace. Today let's make the decision to put these words into action. I guarantee that you'll feel more peaceful than you did yesterday.

Today I resolve to turn away from sin and toward you, Jesus. Thank you for reaching out to me first.

FEBRUARY 20

I thank my God always when I remember
you in my prayers. (Philemon 1:4)

Not exactly a go-to source for those of us who are anxious,
St. Paul's letter to Philemon provides us with this powerful gem, which can actually be very comforting. In this
extremely short epistle, Paul expresses the "joy and comfort" (Philemon 1:7) that resulted from his friendship with
Philemon.

Who is your Philemon? Thinking back over the course
of your life, you've probably had many such friends. God
is constantly blessing us with individuals who comfort and
help us. Let's make it a point to pause and remember them
today. Then, like St. Paul, let's thank God for these people
and ask him to bless them.

Thank you for the many people whom
you have placed in my life, God. Please
bless them abundantly today.

FEBRUARY 21

And let the peace of Christ rule in your hearts,
to which indeed you were called in the one
body. And be thankful. (Colossians 3:15)

Do you let the peace of Christ rule in your heart? Better yet, do you even believe it's possible to be peaceful in this crazy world? Obviously it is possible or St. Paul wouldn't be instructing the people of Colossae to do it. A careful reading of this verse will reveal the secret to making it a reality.

When we are baptized we become part of the mystical body of Christ, the Church. Because of that Christ's peace is very attainable—unless we let the problems of the world distract us. How can we avoid being distracted? If you learn to appreciate the many blessings in your life (including the fact that you are alive and can read this), the little annoyances will seem more trivial and the peace of Christ will truly rule in your heart.

Thank you for all your gifts, God. Focusing on
them allows your peace to rule in my heart.

FEBRUARY 22

If any of you lacks wisdom, let him ask God,
who gives to all men generously and without
reproaching, and it will be given him. (James 1:5)

Over the years I've asked God for many things, but rarely have I asked for wisdom. When it comes to our prayer requests, wisdom and other spiritual needs generally take a backseat to material requests. In this verse St. James assures us that God will grant us wisdom whenever we ask for it. Why would he single out this particular gift? Because it's very important!

According to the *Catechism of the Catholic Church*, wisdom is a spiritual gift that enables one to know the purpose and plan of God (see *CCC* 1831). St. Thomas Aquinas considered it to be the greatest of the gifts of the Holy Spirit. Are you trying to figure out how God can bring good out of the suffering in your life? This verse provides the answer. Ask for more wisdom today!

God, today above all please grant me
an increase in your gift of wisdom.

FEBRUARY 23

Indeed I count everything as loss because of the surpassing worth of knowing Christ Jesus my Lord. For his sake I have suffered the loss of all things, and count them as refuse, in order that I may gain Christ. (Philippians 3:8)

What are you worried about today? Finances? Possessions? Relationships? Illness? These worldly problems often get blamed for the stress we experience, but are they really to blame?

Don't make the mistake of believing the world's message that you can only be peaceful if you have no problems, because it will never happen. Believe instead that you can experience peace by having a close, personal relationship with Jesus Christ. Continue to pray for your needs, but make it a point to grow closer to Christ each day. Because he had a close relationship with Jesus, St. Paul could write these words while sitting in jail! Even though he had many problems, he knew that Jesus was all he truly needed to be peaceful.

Thank you for being my friend, Jesus.
Please help me to know you better.

FEBRUARY 24

God, the Lord, is my strength; he makes
my feet like deer's feet, he makes me tread
upon my high places. (Habakkuk 3:19)

Are you ready for whatever today will bring? Hopefully you'll meet one pleasant experience after another, but you will probably run into a problem or two. Do you feel strong enough to head out the door and face the world? You should!

The prophet Habakkuk reminds us of an easily forgotten fact: You are not alone. Furthermore, you have someone with you who is all-powerful! The same God who created the universe out of nothing is with you today and every day. No matter what happens to you, God is right beside you. Turn to him often throughout the day and know that whatever you face, you'll face it together!

*Thank you for your constant presence in my
life, Jesus. With you by my side, I can deal
with anything that happens today.*

FEBRUARY 25

"I am the vine, you are the branches. He who abides in me, and I in him, he it is that bears much fruit, for apart from me you can do nothing." (John 15:5)

Fear of failure has often caused me to avoid taking on challenges. Thinking I was too weak to get the job done, I have taken a pass on many great opportunities in my life. I realize now that this was a mistake.

While there is nothing wrong with being weak, there is something wrong with not asking for help. Jesus is very clear when he states that we can do nothing without him. *Nothing!* Remember this the next time you face a challenge in your life, but don't stop there. Pay attention to what Jesus said about bearing fruit and turn to him for help. Sometimes Christ asks us to step out of our comfort zones and do something scary. Before you automatically decline, remember his words of assurance and abide in him.

Even though I am weak, Jesus, I know
I can do great things through you.

FEBRUARY 26

He made the storm be still, and the waves
of the sea were hushed. (Psalm 107:29)

When my wife, Eileen, was pregnant with our twin daughters, Mary and Elizabeth, we were faced with a very difficult "storm." The girls were suffering from twin-to-twin transfusion syndrome, an often fatal ailment that affects identical twins in the womb. We prayed for a physical healing, but it was a long shot. Several doctors informed us that the girls would probably not survive. Against all odds, God stilled the storm in our lives and allowed our daughters to live.

Sometimes we mistakenly think that all miracles ceased when Christ ascended into heaven. As a result, we often fail to pray for a miracle. While Jesus doesn't always deliver a miraculous healing or take away our problems, he gives us what we need. He may still the storm—or he may give us a sturdier boat. Let's leave that up to him. In the meantime, don't ever stop seeking his assistance.

God, when the storms are raging and things
look bleak, I choose to trust in you.

FEBRUARY 27

Return to the Lord, your God, for he is gracious and merciful, slow to anger, and abounding in steadfast love, and repents of evil. (Joel 2:13)

God's mercy is something we often take for granted. While I can find dozens of things to complain or worry about each day, I often forget to pause and thank him for being so merciful to me. Over the course of my life, he has forgiven me more times than I could ever count.

Why do we fail to better appreciate God's infinite mercy toward us? I honestly believe it's due to a lack of awareness. Appreciation for God's mercy often gets buried beneath a stack of worries and concerns. Why not change that today? If it weren't for God's mercy, you would never be able to experience the eternal happiness of heaven. Let's stop worrying about our problems for a few minutes and thank him for being so merciful.

Thank you for your unconditional love and mercy, Father. Please grant me the grace to be aware of all you do for me.

FEBRUARY 28

"Therefore do not be anxious about tomorrow, for tomorrow will be anxious for itself. Let the day's own trouble be sufficient for the day." (Matthew 6:34)

As I write this meditation, I'm glancing at a Post-it note with a list of things that I must get done tomorrow. If I dwell on the list too much, panic will set in and today's productivity will go down the drain! Living one day at a time can be challenging, but it's something we must learn to do.

God blessed us with the gift of today, and he expects us to accomplish something. Worrying about what needs to get done tomorrow or what might happen to us in the future is not only useless, but it wastes valuable time needed for today's work. The best way to change this unproductive habit is to ask God for help and to stop yourself as soon as you begin to ruminate on the future. The Lord already has it covered!

Thank you for giving me another day, God. When I begin to worry about the future, instead—with your grace—I'll concentrate on the present moment.

FEBRUARY 29

"And some fell among thorns; and the thorns grew with it and choked it." (Luke 8:7)

In the parable of the sower, Jesus states that not every seed that is planted will grow. He goes on to list three possible reasons for this occurrence. The one that always gets my attention is the seed being choked by thorns.

When questioned by his disciples, Christ explains that the seed that falls among the thorns represents "those who hear, but as they go on their way they are choked by the cares and riches and pleasures of life, and their fruit does not mature" (Luke 8:14).

Be careful. Those cares of life that cause you so much anxiety can be deadly. Make it a point to pause and spend some time in prayer today. Doing so will greatly increase your chances of bearing fruit and ending up in heaven.

Jesus, I am worried about many things today, but
I know my first priority is spending time with
you. You are more important than anything.

MARCH 1

God spoke of old to our fathers by the prophets;
but in these last days he has spoken to us by a Son,
whom he appointed the heir of all things, through
whom also he created the ages. (Hebrews 1:1–2)

We are very blessed to be living in the present age. Even though we can become frustrated by the state of the world and the constant barrage of information thrust upon us each day, we have something that our ancient ancestors did not have. We have Jesus and his Catholic Church.

For many generations God was a mysterious figure to his people. That all changed two thousand years ago when the Word became flesh and became man. Through his Church Jesus provides us with the grace and the knowledge that we need to get to heaven. As an unworthy sinner who tends to become anxious when confused, I find this very comforting. The Church has what we need to navigate the treacherous roads of life.

Thank you for being present in the Church, Jesus.
Grant me the grace to always follow her teachings.

MARCH 2

Abraham was a hundred years old when his son Isaac was born to him. (Genesis 21:5)

I never thought I would get married. Even though I always had a desire to be a husband and father, I was very shy, and dating was not easy for me. By the time I turned thirty, I had just about given up on finding a spouse. But I kept praying.

When I was thirty-four, I met my future wife, Eileen, and we were married one year later. As I reflect on this great blessing, I recognize it as a miracle. It wasn't luck, it wasn't due to hard work on my part—it was God miraculously intervening in my life and doing something I had thought was impossible.

God told Abraham that he would have many descendants, and Abraham believed. Even though it wasn't looking good, Abraham continued to believe and God eventually delivered. He can do the same thing in your life. Don't lose hope!

God, help me never lose sight of your infinite power. With you, all things are possible!

MARCH 3

Have you ever had to do something frightening and dreaded the fact that you had to do it alone? Suddenly a friend offers to accompany you and it doesn't seem quite as bad. As nice as it is to have the company, it's even better if your friend is somehow able to help you with the task. When I bought my first house, for example, my parents came with me and greatly decreased my level of anxiety.

Life can be challenging, especially when it comes to spiritual matters. We are surrounded with temptation and Satan knows our weaknesses. On the surface it seems like the odds of making it to heaven are slim. Fortunately we're not fighting the battle on our own. Jesus is with us every day, and he gives us the grace to emerge victorious. With him we can overcome any challenge that life throws at us—even the booby traps set by the evil one.

Today, Father, lead me not into
temptation. Jesus, I trust in you!

MARCH 4

And the Lord said, "If you had faith as a grain of mustard seed, you could say to this sycamine tree, 'Be rooted up, and be planted in the sea,' and it would obey you." (Luke 17:6)

Considering how many times Jesus refers to the importance of faith in the Bible, it's easy to see why we can become anxious if we feel that our faith is weak. If you read between the lines, however, his words should make you feel better.

Faith is a gift and we receive it (along with hope and charity) when we are baptized. Because it is a gift, we can't just go out and get more of it by ourselves. While we can (and should) pray for a stronger faith, it's impossible to just force ourselves to believe. Is there anything else we can do? Yes! Instead of dwelling on your weak faith, try using what little you have. The results will amaze you.

Jesus, today I will use whatever faith I have,
no matter how small. By doing so, I'll give you
the chance to do great things in my life.

MARCH 5

But Jonah rose to flee to Tarshish from
the presence of the Lord. (Jonah 1:3)

Doing God's will is easy—that is, when it's comfortable! Sometimes, however, God wants us to step out of our comfort zones. There have been many times in my life when I have tried to run away from what God wanted me to do, thinking it would be too painful. In every case, however, running away proved to be more painful than what I was being asked to do.

Jonah did not want to go to Nineveh. Even though God wanted him to preach a message of repentance to the Ninevites, Jonah wanted no part of it and tried to escape. When that didn't work, he discovered that it's much easier to go along with God's plan than to run away from it. That is good advice for each of us.

God, I know that following your will
today will bring me peace even if
I'm outside my comfort zone.

MARCH 6

"Blessed are the poor in spirit, for theirs is the kingdom of heaven." (Matthew 5:3)

A few years ago I attended a men's fellowship meeting at my parish and the beatitudes were being discussed. As soon as this verse was read, confusion filled the room. Is Jesus actually suggesting that our spiritual life should be poor? Not at all!

In the first of the beatitudes, Jesus is stressing the importance of spiritual poverty. That is when we recognize that everything we have is a gift and that we should be willing to give it up if necessary. It doesn't mean that we must get rid of all of our possessions, but that we should place God first in our lives. Nothing should get in the way of our relationship with him. When we take into consideration that worrying about losing our earthly treasures is a big source of stress, his advice makes a great deal of sense. Putting his words into practice will greatly reduce your anxiety level.

Today I recognize that everything I have is a gift from you, Jesus. Help me to never forget it.

MARCH 7

And God saw everything that he had made,
and behold, it was very good. (Genesis 1:31)

When we're struggling, it's easy to become negative. As we look around us, we see nothing but gloom and doom. If we aren't careful, every glass of water that we encounter will be half-empty instead of half-full. Not only is this guaranteed to bring us misery, but it causes us to reject one of God's gifts: the gift of joy.

Everything that God created is good. There are no exceptions. If something or someone doesn't appear to be good, it is an illusion. In order for us to believe this absolute truth, however, we will have to remind ourselves several times each day. Anything that happens today or anyone you meet can somehow help you to grow closer to God. Even if it doesn't feel like it, it's still true!

*God, today I choose to see the good in everything
that happens to me and everyone I meet.*

MARCH 8

And this is the confidence which we have in him, that if we ask anything according to his will he hears us. (1 John 5:14)

I had a psychology professor in college who asked us to try an interesting experiment. He suggested that the next time we're talking with someone on the phone, we observe what happens when we only answer direct questions. I tried this with a friend of mine and, as expected, it drove him crazy.

At one time or another, most of us have questioned if God is really listening to our prayers. It usually happens when he doesn't respond fast enough or when he says no. No matter how we feel, God sees everything we do and always hears our prayers. Sometimes he remains silent, however, so that we'll learn to trust him more. Let's keep this in mind today. If he was willing to become man, suffer, and die for us, why would he turn a deaf ear to our cries for help?

I know that you hear me when I cry out to you, Jesus. Help me to remember that, even when you are silent.

MARCH 9

Good things and bad, life and death, poverty and wealth, come from the Lord. (Sirach 11:14)

Why do bad things happen? Is it because God wants us to suffer or because he doesn't care about us? While many people feel this way, it is completely inconsistent with an all-loving Father. If God truly loves us, all his actions will reflect that love. And they do!

As a human being I will never be able to fully understand God's actions. Even with my very limited intelligence, however, I can look back over my life and see "bad" happenings that produced very positive results. Although I didn't see the value at the time, sickness, unemployment, and loneliness have all brought me closer to God.

God knows what you need to grow closer to him, and he will let these things happen in your life. Even if there is pain involved, whatever happens to you today will contain an unseen message from him: "I love you."

Thank you for loving me so much, Father.
Help me to view all that happens to me
today as an expression of your love.

MARCH 10

And when Jesus heard it, he said to them, "Those who are well have no need of a physician, but those who are sick; I came not to call the righteous, but sinners." (Mark 2:17)

I have a confession to make. Even though I try to follow Jesus and avoid sin, I fall on my face more often than I'd like to admit. While this used to be very discouraging, I have learned to look at it differently. Every time I fall I am reminded of just how much I need God's help.

Jesus wants us to do what we can to avoid sin, but he doesn't expect us to do it on our own. He wants us to ask for the grace to be holy and then to cooperate with that grace. What a pity it would be if we forgot how much we need his help and somehow thought that we were doing it all by ourselves. Try keeping this in mind the next time you fall.

I can't do anything without your help, Jesus.
Thank you for not leaving me to my own devices!

MARCH 11

I consider that the sufferings of this present time are not worth comparing with the glory that is to be revealed to us. (Romans 8:18)

It's a comforting thought to know that the future will be better than the present. In fact, that belief is what motivates many people to get out of bed in the morning. As pleasing as it is to know that things will get better, it's even more comforting to know that the future will be *so much better* that it's not even worth comparing it to the present.

In his letter to the Romans, St. Paul delivers a message that we need to hear every day. This Bible verse is definitely worthy of being marked with a yellow highlighter. It is an expression of Christian hope. No matter how much you are suffering now, a great reward has been prepared for you in heaven. And it's so good that it's not even worth comparing to anything that you experience in this life.

Dear God, as I struggle with challenging situations today, keep me focused on the eternal happiness that awaits me in heaven.

MARCH 12

For thus says the Lord to the house of Israel: "Seek me and live." (Amos 5:4)

We seek many things over the course of our lives. Whether we realize it or not, our daily actions are generally driven by the pursuit of such things as comfort, peace, wealth, recognition, friendship, and pleasure. In moderation these things are fine, but sometimes they aren't good for us—and they can even be dangerous, especially when it comes to our relationship with God.

I am known for my talks on overcoming anxiety, but my goal is actually much broader than that. My main objective is to bring souls closer to Christ. If all I did was teach people how to stop worrying and I didn't bring God into the picture, I would be doing them a great disservice. I want you to stop worrying and so does Jesus, but it is critical that you don't lose sight of the big picture. We should strive to grow closer to Christ each day. Doing so will not only bring us peace, but will move us closer to our eternal reward.

I will seek you, God, with my whole heart.
Let nothing ever come between us.

MARCH 13

"Peace I leave with you; my peace I give to you; not as the world gives do I give to you. Let not your hearts be troubled, neither let them be afraid." (John 14:27)

Isn't it great to feel peaceful? Unfortunately, the problems we face each day often rob us of our peace. How can we learn to experience the peace of Christ when we're constantly bombarded with problems?

The peace that Jesus gives us does not depend on external circumstances. His supernatural peace can be felt even in the midst of great suffering. If all we do is seek solutions to our earthly problems, we'll end up like dogs chasing their tails. We'll never be successful. Instead we should make it a point to seek Jesus every day and ensure that our relationship with him is thriving. That will bring us the lasting peace that he wants us to have.

Jesus, too often external things steal my peace.
But you show me that life doesn't have to be
problem-free in order to experience your peace.
Difficult situations are great opportunities to exercise
my trust in you. I know that with you by my side, I
can be peaceful no matter what happens in my life.

MARCH 14

God is faithful, and he will not let you be tempted
beyond your strength, but with the temptation
will also provide the way of escape, that you
may be able to endure it. (1 Corinthians 10:13)

There have been times in my life when I've felt like I was
at the end of my rope. On many occasions I have cried out
to God and begged him to take away my problems because
I couldn't take it anymore. Sometimes the problem disappeared and sometimes it didn't, but somehow I'm still here
to write about it.

Here's something you can take to the bank: God will
never give you more than you can handle. The fact that
you're reading this confirms that none of your problems
have killed you thus far. Keep this in mind as you move forward with the rest of your life. God loves you and only wants
what is best for you. If he allows something painful to happen, there is a reason for it. By all means ask God to put an
end to your suffering—but then accept his answer. He will
give you the grace you need to endure.

Sometimes I forget just how much you love me,
Father. Help me to remember that you will never
give me more suffering than I can handle.

MARCH 15

Return, O faithless children, says the Lord;
for I am your master; I will take you, one
from a city and two from a family, and I
will bring you to Zion. (Jeremiah 3:14)

Even though I have turned my back on him many times over the years, God has never given up on me. While I was busy seeking fleeting pleasure, he waited patiently and kept calling me to return to him. Eventually I stopped fighting and listened to him.

Sometimes we think instant gratification is the only way to happiness. Even though we know that what we're doing is wrong, it feels good and brings us temporary relief from the stress in our lives. But then we have to deal with the guilt that follows. That guilt is God's voice telling you that there is another way. And his way will bring you happiness that will last, with no guilt involved. Don't waste your time seeking instant pleasure that will soon fade. Seek God and the lasting peace that only he can give. I guarantee you'll never regret it.

God, thank you for being patient with me.
Increase my desire to always follow your will.

MARCH 16

Then King David went in and sat before the Lord, and said, "Who am I, O Lord God, and what is my house, that you have brought me thus far?" (2 Samuel 7:18)

Learning to be grateful is one of the shortest paths to happiness. If you develop an "attitude of gratitude," your problems will seem less intimidating, and you will be at peace. Sounds simple, doesn't it?

While this concept is simple in theory, it can be difficult to put into practice because we tend to focus on our problems instead of our blessings. King David understood that he didn't deserve what he received from God. We would be wise to take a page out of his book and do the same. Everything that we have is a gift from God. Possessions, health, life, intelligence, faith, the air that we breathe, and the promise of heaven are all gifts from God. We did nothing to earn them. Spending more time thinking about this will increase your appreciation for God's goodness and decrease your anxiety level.

Thank you for blessing me with so many gifts, God. Please help me to better appreciate all that you do for me.

MARCH 17

> Blessed is the man who endures trial, for
> when he has stood the test he will receive
> the crown of life which God has promised
> to those who love him. (James 1:12)

Do you feel blessed when you endure trials? Well, you are! Even though it might not feel like it, the difficulties that we face each day are blessings in disguise. But even though we can benefit greatly from our suffering, we can also waste it. It all depends on how we respond.

When St. James refers to our trials as blessings, he is implying that we make use of them. If all I do is complain about my suffering, it will do me no good at all. In fact, it will have a negative effect and cause me to be miserable. If, on the other hand, I offer up my pain and use it to draw me closer to Christ, it will bear great fruit.

The problems you are dealing with can help you and others to get to heaven. Ask God for the grace to deal with them in the best way possible.

Thank you for the grace to deal with the problems
in my life, Father, and to see them from your
perspective. Even though it's hard for me to say it,
thank you for allowing me to face these trials.

MARCH 18

In his hands are the depths of the
earth; the heights of the mountains
are his also. (Psalm 95:4)

Have you thought about the fact that God holds the world in his hands? If not, you really should. This simple concept, as expressed by the psalmist in this verse, reminds us that God can do anything he wants to do. This includes working a miracle in your life.

Take a look around you. If God hadn't willed it, you would not be alive, the sun would not have risen, and the world would cease to exist. Thinking about this makes finding a job, paying your bills, or dealing with a serious crisis a little less intimidating. God is always in control and can bring good out of any situation. Keeping this in mind will help you to pray with greater confidence. If you don't believe that God is all-powerful, your prayers will be weak. God can do anything. Remember this the next time you pray!

Thank you for holding the world in your
hands, God. It's reassuring to know that you
are in control of all that concerns me!

MARCH 19

When Joseph woke from sleep,
he did as the angel of the Lord
commanded him. (Matthew 1:24)

While it's true that we don't know much about the life of St. Joseph, this verse tells us all we need to know. Despite the fact that not a single word of his was recorded in the Bible, his actions speak louder than words. I'll go as far as to say that if you follow his example every day of your life, you will not only have great peace, but you will spend eternity in heaven!

We have a tendency to overcomplicate life. In our pursuit of happiness, we often ignore the one thing that will allow us to achieve it: following God's will. St. Joseph knew what it was like to rise above his fears and do the right thing. He knows what it's like to follow God's plan even when it doesn't make sense. He also knows that saying yes to God brings great peace. He wants to help you. Turn to him today.

Good St. Joseph, please pray that I will have the strength to follow God's will even when I'm afraid.

MARCH 20

I am the Lord your God from the land of Egypt; you know no God but me, and besides me there is no savior. (Hosea 13:4)

As an anxious child, I developed many ways to deal with stress. For the most part I sought relief by doing "fun" activities—spending time with my friends, watching TV, playing with toys, and reading comic books. By doing these things I would temporarily forget about my worries. As I grew into an anxious adult, I pursued different activities (hanging out in bars, listening to music, spending money), but my goal was the same. Instead of dealing with the stressors in my life, I tried to run away from them. It didn't work.

After becoming frustrated with living in a perpetual state of anxiety, I finally tried turning to Jesus. And I'm not just talking about turning to him in theory, but *really* turning to him every day. It took me a long time, but I have finally discovered that it is impossible to find lasting peace without having a personal relationship with Jesus Christ. All the diversions and activities in the world won't make your anxiety disappear. He will not only save you from your sins, but he can help you to stop worrying.

Jesus, I turn my life over to you. Help me to break free from worrying.

MARCH 21

*Give thanks to the Lord, for he is good, for
his mercy endures for ever. (Daniel 3:67)*

These are hardly the words one would expect to hear from someone who was standing in the middle of a life-threatening situation, but that's exactly where they were spoken. Filled with anger because of their refusal to worship a golden idol, King Nebuchadnezzar ordered Shadrach, Meshach, and Abednego to be thrown into a blazing fire and burned to death. Because of God's miraculous intervention, however, their lives were spared, and they gave thanks to him while still in the midst of the dangerous flames.

Offering prayers of thanksgiving is not the first thing that comes to mind when facing a crisis, but it's a very good idea. In his mercy God has delivered us from eternal death and made it possible for us to live with him in heaven. No matter how hot the flames surrounding us get, this will not change.

*Thank you for being so merciful to
me, Lord. I am very grateful.*

MARCH 22

On that day it shall be said to Jerusalem:
"Do not fear, O Zion; let not your hands
grow weak." (Zephaniah 3:16)

One of my biggest challenges is remembering just how much Jesus wants to help me. As someone who likes to get things done, I have a tendency to forget to ask for his help. For years I struggled to become more patient, love my enemies, pray when I didn't feel like it, and have a greater trust in God. I was not very successful. Eventually I realized I was trying to do it all on my own and neglecting to ask for God's help.

The prophet *Zephaniah* reminds us that we have no need to fear, even if we are weak. God is in our midst and is patiently waiting for us to turn to him. If you're struggling to overcome a habitual sin or be kind to an annoying coworker, ask him to help you. If you want to stop worrying or grow closer to Jesus, don't try to do it on your own. God is right beside you, and he wants to help.

God, sometimes I get so overwhelmed by my
problems that I forget to turn to you for help.
Please help me to remember that you are right
beside me, waiting to come to my aid.

MARCH 23

Wakefulness over wealth wastes away one's flesh, and anxiety over it removes sleep. (Sirach 31:1)

Did you ever notice that your problems seem worse in the middle of the night? There's something about the darkness that has a tendency to turn molehills into mountains. And if I were to take a survey, I would be willing to bet that financial concerns are a huge source of nighttime worrying.

God is well aware that we need money to survive in this life, but there is a danger to placing too much emphasis on wealth. If we're not careful, our bank account can replace God as our source of security. As a result, stock market declines and unexpected bills can make us very anxious. Let's pray for the wisdom to realize that our security comes from God. Unlike our account balances, which can fluctuate daily, God is the same yesterday, today, and forever!

Help me to remember that my true security lies in you, God.

MARCH 24

And he awoke and rebuked the wind, and said
to the sea, "Peace! Be still!" And the wind
ceased, and there was a great calm. (Mark 4:39)

Sometimes it really does seem like Jesus is sleeping. And to make matters worse, his nap time often takes place during our greatest crises. What are we supposed to do when our world is crumbling and Jesus is asleep?

In order to manage this frustrating problem, we need to understand something about Jesus. He is a deep sleeper and can be difficult to wake up! As a result we need to be very persistent. All kidding aside, we need to understand that God's silence doesn't mean he isn't listening. He is very aware of all the problems we are facing, but sometimes he remains silent so we can learn to trust him more. He wants us to cry out to him for help and even "shake" him if necessary. When the time is right, he will wake up and calm the storm in your life.

*Jesus, I know that you are always aware of what is
going on in my life. I will be persistent in seeking
you, especially when it seems like you are sleeping.*

MARCH 25

And he came to her and said, "Hail, full of grace, the Lord is with you!" (Luke 1:28)

The first words of the angel Gabriel to the Blessed Mother are simple but powerful. After acknowledging her sinlessness, Gabriel delivered a message we all need to hear and believe.

We sometimes mistakenly assume that Mary was given all the answers up front. The fact that she was "greatly troubled" by the preceding greeting and "considered in her mind what sort of a greeting this might be" proves that she didn't know everything. Just like us, Mary dealt with uncertainty in her life. Because she knew God was with her, however, she willingly said yes to the request to become the mother of the Messiah.

Mary knows what it's like to be confused. She is your mother and wants to help you. Turn to her whenever you become overwhelmed with uncertainty in your life.

Mary, thank you for saying yes to God's request even though you faced much uncertainty. Because of your trust, the Savior entered the world, and I am grateful. Help me to trust God as much as you did. Thank you for being my mother!

MARCH 26

"Shall we receive good at the hand of God, and shall we not receive evil?" (Job 2:10)

What in the world is Job talking about? How could evil come from God, who is all good? As shocking as these words are, I can assure you that he makes a great point. Furthermore, accepting this concept can bring you incredible peace.

Most of us react in the same way when we hear the news of a sudden death, unexpected illness, or unemployment. While "That's too bad," "I'm sorry to hear that," and "How sad!" are all very appropriate and compassionate responses to unpleasant events, we should recognize that these responses are also incomplete. Nothing happens to us without God's approval, and he can bring good out of any situation. Accepting this will bring you a great deal of peace. God loves you, and everything that happens to you is an expression of that love . . . even if it hurts.

Thank you for always giving me what I need, God. Today I choose to accept all that happens to me as an expression of your love.

MARCH 27

Blessed be the God of all comfort, who comforts us in all our affliction, so that we may be able to comfort those who are in any affliction, with the comfort with which we ourselves are comforted by God. (2 Corinthians 1:3–4)

I don't like to admit it, but I can be very self-centered at times. Although it's not intentional, I sometimes get so caught up in my problems that I forget about the needs of others. If I'm not careful, I can move from one problem to the next without ever stopping to think that I can help someone else.

In this passage St. Paul reminds us that we should make an effort to bring God's consolation to those who are suffering. We are surrounded with people who are living in misery and don't know that Jesus can help them. Let's do something to change that.

Thank you for consoling me in my suffering, Jesus. Help me to become more aware of the suffering of others, and grant me the wisdom and desire to help them.

MARCH 28

And Gideon said to him, "Please, sir, if the Lord is with us, why then has all this befallen us? And where are all his wonderful deeds?' But now the Lord has cast us off, and given us into the hand of Midian." (Judges 6:13)

At some point in time, most of us have questioned God about the events happening in our lives. Just like Gideon, we may wonder why so many bad things are happening to us. Shouldn't having God on our side produce better results?

When confused, it's perfectly acceptable to ask God questions. While he sometimes provides an explanation, he may remain silent and ask you to trust him. When that happens, take comfort in the fact that he is working in your life and something great is in store for you!

God, please help me to understand when
life seems confusing. I long to have a
greater trust in your providence.

MARCH 29

*"I have come as light into the world,
that whoever believes in me may not
remain in darkness." (John 12:46)*

Indoor lighting is a great thing, isn't it? If I wake up in the middle of the night, it allows me to see clearly in the darkness. But as great as this invention is, it can't help me at all unless I take action. In order for the light to shine in the darkness, I need to flip the switch and turn it on.

Jesus Christ is the light of the world; he became man so we would not have to live in darkness. Because he respects our free will, however, he will not force us to walk in his light. Some action is required on our part. We must invite him to enter our lives and illuminate our path. If you haven't done this, I urge you to do it today. With Christ as your light, you will never again walk in the darkness.

*Jesus, I invite you into my life this day. Please
reveal yourself to me and illuminate my path.*

MARCH 30

Jealousy and anger shorten life, and anxiety brings on old age too soon. (Sirach 30:24)

Despite the world being filled with people who worry, I have yet to meet someone who enjoys being a worrier. Instead of just accepting it as a way of life, however, let's focus on the negative effects of anxiety.

Aside from the fact that anxiety can ruin your enjoyment of the present moment and get in the way of your relationship with God, it can also make you sick. Over the years, I have suffered from many anxiety-related ailments. Heart palpitations, irritable bowel syndrome, shingles, and sleep deprivation have all been part of my life. According to studies, all of these conditions can be caused or aggravated by stress.

Despite all of the negative effects, many of us continue to live with our anxiety. Why? Often it's because we think there is no solution. But there *is* a solution to the problem, and his name is Jesus Christ. Reach out to him today.

I don't want to be controlled by anxiety
any longer, Jesus. I want to stop worrying
and experience your peace.

MARCH 31

And my God will supply every need of
yours according to his riches in glory
in Christ Jesus. (Philippians 4:19)

What does it mean to be rich? Even though the first thing that comes to mind is having an abundance of money, we can also be rich in other ways. Good friends, closeness to God, and hope for the future can make even those living in poverty feel rich.

While we all have material needs, we shouldn't lose sight of the fact that we have spiritual needs as well. Most of us could use a little more joy, hope, and peace in our lives. When was the last time you asked for these spiritual gifts? Today would be a good day to begin asking God for an increase in those treasures that will not perish when we die. And according to the inspired words of St. Paul, God is prepared to supply them to us!

Lord, in addition to all the material blessings
you've provided for me, thank you for the
abundance of spiritual riches that are mine today.

APRIL 1

Blessed be the God and Father of our Lord Jesus Christ! By his great mercy we have been born anew to a living hope through the resurrection of Christ Jesus from the dead. (1 Peter 1:3)

Congratulations! Because of your heavenly Father's mercy, you have been redeemed. Therefore it is possible for you to experience the joy of eternal life in his kingdom. What is even more incredible is that you and I did nothing to earn this gift. It is simply an expression of God's love for us.

As we deal with our problems and duties today, there is a very good chance that we will forget about God's mercy. The distractions of life can cause us to overlook what really matters. Jesus loves you and gave his life so that you can live with him forever. Does anything else matter?

Thank you for redeeming me, Jesus, and for your abundant mercy and love.

APRIL 2

Now the Lord said to Abram, "Go from your country and your kindred and your father's house to the land that I will show you." (Genesis 12:1)

I am a cautious traveler. Before I leave on a trip, I plan out my route. If I am driving I always search the Internet for the best route and print out a copy of the directions so I know what to expect. In addition I make sure my GPS is ready to go. Doing this makes me feel confident that I will reach my destination in a timely manner.

When called by God, Abram wasn't given the luxury of knowing where he was going. He would be given that information at the proper time. Is God asking you to travel an unfamiliar road right now? Are you facing an uncertain future? Look at it as an opportunity to trust him. Instead of focusing on the uncertainty, ask God for the strength to trust him with your life. It worked out for Abram, and it will work out for you.

Father, help me to trust you with the
uncertainty that I face each day.

APRIL 3

"But seek first his kingdom and his righteousness, and all of these things shall be yours as well." (Matthew 6:33)

Do you feel uncomfortable praying for money? You shouldn't. Jesus wants us to depend on him for all our needs, both material and spiritual. He understands that we have financial needs, and he wants to help us with them. As important as these needs are, however, they shouldn't be our main priority in life.

If we are lacking certain virtues, a financial windfall could lead to greed and complacency. Ultimately this could prove to be disastrous on a spiritual level. Thankfully God will sometimes withhold material gifts until we can better handle them. If you are struggling financially, ask the Holy Spirit to reveal your spiritual needs, and then proceed to pray for them. In his wisdom God will satisfy your needs in the proper order.

Holy Spirit, I ask you to reveal my spiritual needs and fill them.

APRIL 4

When the cares of my heart are many, your consolations cheer my soul. (Psalm 94:19)

It is a common belief that joy and problems cannot coexist. As a result we look for ways to run away from or eliminate the difficulties in our lives. Since that only works temporarily at best, we can end up spending many days in complete misery. Fortunately there is a solution to this problem, and it has nothing to do with the elimination of our worldly troubles.

This verse reminds us that Jesus is waiting to console us, especially when we have many cares. He wants us to run into his open arms instead of running from our problems. Like a good friend who provides a shoulder to cry on, Jesus is always available. We can encounter him through Scripture, prayer, and the sacraments. These encounters will reveal the power of his consoling touch and allow us to feel the joy only he can give.

Thank you for your constant willingness to console me, Jesus. Today I will run to you and focus on you instead of my problems.

APRIL 5

We were buried therefore with him by baptism into death, so that as Christ was raised from the dead by the glory of the Father, we too might walk in newness of life. (Romans 6:4)

For many of us the day of our baptism is a distant memory and not something we think about on a regular basis. St. Paul's words to the Romans, however, provide some serious food for thought. While the "dying with Christ" part may not instantly lift your spirits, the message about the newness of life should make you feel pretty good.

Just as it was necessary for Jesus to suffer and die before rising from the dead, we must face struggles and death before we enter heaven. Our journey home begins with the day of our baptism. And while we will have some bad days along the way, the final destination will definitely be worth the pain!

Jesus, please help me to keep my suffering in perspective. Grant me the strength I need to persevere, especially when I am weary.

APRIL 6

Does a man harbor anger against another, and yet seek for healing from the Lord? (Sirach 28:3)

We can sometimes be our own worst enemy, especially when it comes to getting over a past hurt. There have been times in my life when I have been so angry over an offense committed against me that I couldn't sleep. And instead of doing something productive while I tossed and turned, I would replay the incident over and over in my head. As you might expect, I did not feel peaceful.

If you lack peace because of a wrong perpetrated against you, I would strongly suggest that you pray for your offender. You may still be holding a grudge and not even realize it. Even though praying for those who have wronged us does not come naturally, it's very effective and can restore your peace in no time. As I have learned, it's very difficult to pray for someone and be angry with that person at the same time.

God, I ask you to bless anyone
who has hurt me in any way.

APRIL 7

The saying is sure and worthy of full acceptance, that Christ Jesus came into the world to save sinners. And I am the foremost of sinners. (1 Timothy 1:15)

I don't know about you, but I typically don't consider St. Paul to be "the foremost of sinners." The fact that he views himself this way illustrates his humility. His statement also reminds us that no matter how much we have sinned in the past, there is hope.

Even though it isn't pleasant to admit, we are all sinners in need of a savior. Jesus Christ came into the world for that very reason. Instead of feeling dejected about the many times you have fallen, rejoice that there is an answer. Through the sacrament of reconciliation, all your sins can be forgiven. Make it a point to receive this great outpouring of God's mercy on a regular basis. It will bring you great peace.

Lord Jesus Christ, Son of God,
have mercy on me, a sinner.

APRIL 8

For she said, "If I touch even his garments,
I shall be made well." (Mark 5:28)

In 1997, while my wife was pregnant, she had an ultrasound to determine if our twins were still alive. During the procedure she suddenly thought of this verse. Making it her own, Eileen pictured herself touching the garments of Jesus and believing that he could heal Mary and Elizabeth of their life-threatening ailment.

While we never know for sure if Jesus will heal someone physically, it's important to believe that he *can*. Otherwise we might just miss out on a miracle. Even though God can do all things, there is actually someone who can block his miraculous power. That someone is you. Don't allow it to happen. Touch his garments today and let his power work in your life.

Help me to believe in your miraculous power,
God, and allow it to work freely in my life.

APRIL 9

Behold, as the eyes of servants look to the hand of their master, as the eyes of a maid to the hand of her mistress, so our eyes look to the Lord our God, till he have mercy upon us. (Psalm 123:2)

As a recovering worrier I am well aware that I can give in to my anxiety at any moment. Unless I'm careful I can easily find myself worrying about any number of issues. Fortunately I have been able to identify my major weakness when it comes to anxiety, and it gets me into trouble every time: taking my eyes off Jesus.

In order to break free from worrying, you and I must make a conscious decision to focus on Jesus throughout the day. Forgetting about him will allow problems and fears to overtake us. Reading the Gospels and speaking to him in prayer will help us to recall his presence. Receiving the sacraments will strengthen our faith even more. Don't make the same mistake I have made so many times. Always keep your eyes on Jesus!

Jesus, help me focus on you
throughout the day today.

APRIL 10

"Fear not, I am the first and the last, and the living one; I died, and behold I am alive for evermore, and I have the keys of Death and Hades." (Revelation 1:17–18)

If you asked one hundred worriers what frightens them the most, I suspect that death would be a very common answer. The finality of death scares many people, but it didn't scare Jesus. Not only did Christ bring people back to life, he rose from the dead himself. If you are afraid to die, Jesus is definitely someone you want to get to know!

Death is not a big deal to Jesus, and that should make you feel good. The *Catechism of the Catholic Church* says, "The obedience of Jesus has transformed the curse of death into a blessing" (*CCC*, 1009). If the thought of death frightens you, try to remember it is not a permanent state. When we die in this life, it opens up a door that leads to eternal life in heaven.

I know that I will die one day, Jesus, but I am frightened. Help me to love you so much that I can't wait to live with you in heaven.

APRIL 11

And he believed the Lord; and he reckoned it to him as righteousness. (Genesis 15:6)

There is a big difference between having faith and being gullible. While both require some degree of trust, having faith also makes use of reason. Even though it was improbable because of his advanced age, Abram believed God's promise of numerous descendants. Looking back we see that his trust was well founded. The Lord never once lied to Abram—and he will never lie to us.

You can search throughout the Bible for one instance when God reneged on his promise, and you'll come up empty. Why then do we spend so much time worrying about what will happen in our lives? If we read through Scripture, we can see that God always delivers on his promises. The greatest example can be found in the person of Jesus Christ, the long-awaited Messiah. Spend some time reflecting on this today. Then you will be able to face the future with confidence, believing that Jesus is worthy of your trust.

Jesus, today I will choose to be more
aware of your trustworthiness instead
of focusing on future concerns.

APRIL 12

Rejoice in the Lord always; again I will
say, Rejoice. (Philippians 4:4)

If you read this verse at a time when nothing is going your way, there is a good chance you will ignore it. After all, why should you rejoice when you're miserable? I can't say for sure, but I suspect that St. Paul considered this and decided to repeat his words for emphasis.

When should we rejoice? Always. Even when we don't feel like it? *Especially* when we don't feel like it! Why should we rejoice? We should rejoice because we were created by an unchanging God who loves us with an unconditional love. If you make it a point to rejoice every day, even when you feel miserable, it will eventually become a habit. And being joyful is one habit you never want to break!

Thank you for loving me so much, Jesus. Thinking
about your goodness makes me want to rejoice!

APRIL 13

But the angel of the Lord came down into the furnace to be with Azariah and his companions, and drove the fiery flame out of the furnace. (Daniel 3:26)

I have lived through many frightening situations. Some were physical, some were spiritual, and some just involved my imagination running wild. Whatever the cause, I'm grateful God allowed me to get through these episodes in one piece.

It's difficult to imagine something more frightening than being burned alive in a furnace. Just thinking about it makes me queasy. That is exactly what happened to Azariah and his companions, however—and they survived. Through the presence of the angel in the furnace, we are reminded that God is with us always. Furthermore he has given you a guardian angel to keep you safe from spiritual danger. If you haven't spoken to your guardian angel, make it a point to introduce yourself today.

Angel of God, my guardian dear,
To whom God's love commits me here,
Ever this day, be at my side,
To light and guard, to rule and guide. Amen.

APRIL 14

There is no fear in love, but perfect
love casts out fear. (1 John 4:18)

This popular Bible verse often gets taken out of context. Contrary to what some individuals may claim, St. John is not saying that we cannot love God if we are afraid. If that were the case, it would be impossible to explain the biblically documented fear felt by Abraham, Moses, St. Joseph, St. Paul, and the Blessed Mother.

In a discussion of the final judgment (see 1 John 4:17–19), St. John mentions that if we love God, we have no reason to be afraid of that important event. We will all die and be judged, but those who love God will view that day with anticipation, not dread.

At this point you are still alive and can make an effort to better love God. Instead of worrying about how you will fare on judgment day, look for ways to love God more while you are still here. As your love for him increases, your fear of judgment will decrease.

Heavenly Father, I look forward to seeing
you when my earthly life has ended. Grant
me the grace to love you more each day.

APRIL 15

He said to them, "It is not for you to know times or seasons which the Father has fixed by his own authority." (Acts 1:7)

When I worked for the federal government, sensitive information was shared on a "need to know" basis. Not every employee had access to all classified information. For example, I was allowed to view only the data necessary to perform my duties.

When asked if he was ready to restore the kingdom to Israel, Jesus told his disciples they didn't need to know that information. In other words, that is the Father's business. Too many times we allow ourselves to be distracted by things that are beyond our control. This can cause us to neglect doing what we are supposed to do. Every day we are expected to make an effort to know, love, and serve God. If we focus on performing those tasks, we'll eventually find out all the other answers—when we get to heaven.

Today I will do my best to know, love,
and serve you, God. Help me to stay
focused on your will for me.

APRIL 16

"And whatever you ask in prayer, you will receive, if you have faith." (Matthew 21:22)

In all honesty this is one of those Bible verses that can either drive you crazy or give you confidence. While it does require some pondering, the message that Jesus delivers in this verse is one you should never forget.

Obviously we know there is more to this message than meets the eye, so we shouldn't take it out of context. Because he loves us, God will never give us anything that could harm us. Jesus is emphasizing the importance of faith. If we don't believe he can truly help us, our prayers will be lacking. As someone who struggled with a weak faith for many years, I'd like to share a piece of advice: Don't underestimate God's power. When you pray, make your intentions big and give him room to work. Your faith will never increase if you don't allow Jesus to perform miracles in your life.

Jesus, please increase my weak faith
so I can trust in you more. Let me
never underestimate your power!

APRIL 17

For a thousand years in your sight are
but as yesterday when it is past, or as
a watch in the night. (Psalm 90:4)

If you would like to be peaceful, I recommend that you accept the fact that God is not in a hurry. And because he knows what is best, all the complaining and tears in the world will not cause him to alter his schedule. It took thousands of years for the Messiah to arrive, so it may take a while for your intentions to be answered.

Whatever you do, don't stop asking for what you need. God wants you to depend on him. He also wants you to be persistent and keep praying even if he seems to be taking a long time to respond. Being God gives him the advantage of knowing the best time to answer your prayers. The passage of time may be a big deal to you, but to God a thousand years is the same as one day.

*Thank you for always knowing the best
time to answer my prayers, God.*

APRIL 18

We are afflicted in every way, but not crushed;
perplexed, but not driven to despair;
persecuted, but not forsaken; struck down,
but not destroyed. (2 Corinthians 4:8–9)

Life certainly has its challenges. From the time we are born until the time we die, we will endure many unpleasant experiences. Nothing that happens to us in this life, however, can change the fact that we were created to live forever in heaven.

St. Paul experienced more than his share of suffering, but he never lost sight of the big picture. He understood that all the unpleasant things that happened in his life were rungs on the ladder leading to heaven. Even though it can be difficult, keep this in mind as you encounter various obstacles in your life. By turning to Christ you can receive the grace to deal with anything that comes your way.

I give you the challenges I will face today, Jesus. Even
though it's difficult to see, I know everything that
happens in my life can help me to grow closer to you.

APRIL 19

"Yet it was I who taught Ephraim to walk, I took them up in my arms; but they did not know that I healed them." (Hosea 11:3)

How has God blessed you today? If you are struggling to come up with an answer, let me offer some suggestions. If you are reading this, you have the ability to see. In order for you to be alive, the organs in your body have to work in perfect harmony, without any help from you. Once again today the sun came up and the world continued to exist. I could go on, but I think you get the idea.

We are blessed in so many ways that we can easily become desensitized. The main reason we are not happy is that we lose sight of God's presence in our lives. Without his approval we would cease to exist. He wills our every breath and makes it possible for us to speak and think. Spend a few minutes thinking about that today.

Heavenly Father, thank you for the many ways you bless me each day. Help me to be more aware of your presence in my life.

APRIL 20

"He is not here; for he has risen,
as he said." (Matthew 28:6)

Aside from the fact that it confirms Christ's resurrection, this verse is important for another reason. The angel's words reveal that Jesus doesn't lie. If he says he will do something, you can count on him to follow through. While I've been disappointed many times by people not doing what they said they would do, I am very grateful Jesus is so reliable.

If Jesus came through on his promise of rising from the dead, what will stop him from doing all the other things he promised? Therefore we can be assured of his constant presence in our lives and be confident there is a place prepared for us in heaven. Whenever life becomes burdensome, remembering these promises should bring us comfort. Make no mistake about it—Jesus is good for his word!

*Thank you for being so reliable, Jesus. Your
constant presence in my life is the best
cure for worry and discouragement.*

APRIL 21

> Be sober, be watchful. Your adversary the
> devil prowls around like a roaring lion
> seeking some one to devour. (1 Peter 5:8)

This is hardly a verse you would expect to find in a book designed to help you find peace, but it expresses a message you need to hear. Satan is real, and he wants to keep you from doing God's will. One of his favorite tactics is to play on your fears.

Almost everything God asks us to do involves some level of fear. Volunteering at church, helping the poor, sharing the Good News, and trusting in divine providence can all cause some level of fear or uncertainty. Fearing a negative outcome or bad experience, we sometimes avoid doing what God calls us to do. This is exactly what Satan wants. Don't believe his lies. If God asks you to do something, he will never desert you.

Jesus, today I will be alert to Satan's
tactics that cause me to fear and doubt.
Please protect me from him today.

APRIL 22

"Arise, go to Zarephath, which belongs to Sidon, and dwell there. Behold, I have commanded a widow there to feed you." (1 Kings 17:9)

God had previously instructed the prophet Elijah to go to a region east of the Jordan River. While the prophet was at this location, God supplied all his needs. Ravens brought him food, and a brook provided drinking water. But then the brook dried up, and Elijah was given a new set of instructions.

It's been said that the one constant in life is change. Those of us who have experienced death, illness, financial struggles, and job loss see the truth in this statement. In reality, however, there is one thing that never changes: God! Even though our lives can be filled with instability, he is always there to provide. Elijah trusted in God's providence and wasn't disappointed. If you follow the prophet's example, you'll see how he will provide for your needs as well.

Father in heaven, give us this day our daily bread.

APRIL 23

"Fear not, little flock, for it is your Father's good pleasure to give you the kingdom." (Luke 12:32)

Several years ago I went to the store to purchase my first smartphone. Thinking I could not afford the model I really wanted, I inquired about an inferior phone that I thought would be more in my price range. I was stunned when the clerk revealed that my first choice was actually the cheaper of the two. Sometimes it's not good to settle for less.

Because we are material creatures, we rely on our senses. This can be problematic if it leads to too much emphasis on accumulating earthly possessions. Just because we can see and touch these things doesn't automatically make them important. Although invisible, the treasures of heaven are more important than all the money and possessions in the world. Don't settle for what this world has to offer. Start filling up your heavenly treasure chest today!

Jesus, help me to realize that my true security
lies in you and the treasures of heaven.

APRIL 24

"Behold, God is my salvation; I will trust and not be afraid; for the Lord God is my strength and my song, and he has become my salvation." (Isaiah 12:2)

Imagine how you would feel if you boarded a plane for a cross country trip and the following announcement was made: "Good morning, ladies and gentlemen, this is your captain speaking. I have never flown a 737 before, and I am totally confused by all these gauges and controls in the cockpit. Can anyone help me figure out how to get this thing off the ground?" Our hypothetical pilot is hardly a person you would want to trust with your life, is he?

The more we learn about God, the more our confidence in him will grow. If we aren't familiar with his power and what he has done in the past, it will be extremely difficult to trust him with our lives. The Bible is filled with stories of ordinary people doing extraordinary things with God's help. Reading these stories will help you learn *about* God, but more important, it will help you to know him *personally*. Then, and only then, will you be able to trust him with your life.

I will trust you with my life, Lord, today and always. Please help me to know you better.

APRIL 25

For this is the will of God, your
sanctification. (1 Thessalonians 4:3)

"What does God want me to do?" This is a question we
should ask ourselves frequently, but we often avoid it because it seems too intimidating. In reality the answer is
much simpler than you might expect.

While God sometimes calls us to perform specific tasks,
his will for our lives can be summed up in this verse from St.
Paul's first letter to the Thessalonians. God wants us to be
holy. Of course, this requires work on our part. Even though
he is ready to provide all the grace we need, we still have to
cooperate with that grace and fight against our desire to sin.

The good news is that you know what he wants you to
do today. There is no need for you to wonder and become
stressed. Wherever you are and whatever you do today, keep
this in mind. No matter how challenging it may seem, it is
possible for you to follow God's will by being holy.

Thank you for revealing your will to me, Father.
Help me to be holy in all that I say and do.

APRIL 26

"Give us this day our daily bread."
(Matthew 6:11)

Why do so many people play the lottery each day, hoping to win millions of dollars? For many the thought of hitting the jackpot provides security. On the surface, waking up each day with no financial worries is a very attractive thought. Unfortunately it's also an easy way to forget about God.

The Lord knows us very well. In fact, he knows us better than we know ourselves. He understands that if we become too secure and complacent, we will quickly forget that we need him in our lives. A look at the history of the Israelites proves this. When things were going well for the chosen people, they had a tendency to forget about God. When things turned sour, however, they suddenly rediscovered their need for his help. There is a reason Jesus instructed us to ask for our *daily* bread, not a lifetime supply. He wants us to turn to him every day of our lives.

Please grant me all that I need this day, Lord.

APRIL 27

"My sheep hear my voice, and I know them, and they follow me." (John 10:27)

How often does Jesus speak to you? Before you dismiss the question as something that doesn't apply to you, I can assure you that he speaks to you frequently every day. The fact that you may not hear him doesn't mean that he isn't speaking. In order to hear Christ's voice, you must learn to listen.

While God speaks in many different ways (Scripture, nature, prayer, other people, circumstances), the main reason we don't hear him is excessive noise. Unless we make a conscious effort to spend some time in silence on a daily basis, we will miss out on hearing what Jesus has to say. Make a commitment to unplug from the world and listen for his voice today. You will be surprised to realize just how much he has to say.

Today I will make sure I unplug from all the noise around me and really listen for your voice. I'm listening, Jesus.

APRIL 28

They will fight against you; but they shall not prevail against you, for I am with you, says the Lord, to deliver you. (Jeremiah 1:19)

I wasn't very good when I played Little League baseball, but our team did have a few players who were quite talented. As could be expected, the manager knew which players to lean on when he needed a win. If it was a close game, putting the right players in the lineup could turn a potential loss into a victory.

In the game of life, you don't have to be a superstar to emerge victorious and make it to heaven. What you do need are the right players on your team. If your lineup includes the angels and saints, you will do well. When you become discouraged, always remember that even though you feel weak, your heavenly teammates can carry you to victory.

Thank you for the gift of the angels and saints, Father. Please remind me to turn to them often.

APRIL 29

By faith Abraham obeyed when he was called
to go out to a place which he was to receive as
an inheritance; and he went out, not knowing
where he was to go. (Hebrews 11:8)

Did you ever feel guilty because you didn't want to help someone? While guilt might be justified if you refused to help, sometimes you feel guilty even when you do the right thing. In cases like this what matters most is how you act, not how you feel.

Trusting God isn't always easy. We are human, and sometimes we struggle to move forward into the unknown. Growing closer to Christ involves stepping out in faith. The fact that Abraham obeyed doesn't mean he wasn't afraid. It means he believed in God's promises. You can do the same . . . even if you feel a little weak in the knees.

God, help me to remember that my actions are more important than my feelings. Increase my desire to follow you always, especially when I am afraid.

APRIL 30

*You are the God who works wonders,
who have manifested your might
among the peoples. (Psalm 77:14)*

When praying, are you sometimes at a loss for words? You are not alone. Having a conversation with God can be very challenging, especially because he is invisible. We can also become so overwhelmed by our problems that we don't know what to say to him.

The most important thing to remember about prayer is that it is a relationship with God. It's more important to say something to him than to rack your brain thinking of the perfect words. If you're looking for a good way to start your prayer, however, this verse provides a great answer. By beginning your prayer in this manner, you not only give God the praise he is due; you also remind yourself that he can work miracles in your life. Not a bad way to start a conversation!

*I am in awe of your power, Jesus. Thank you for
your willingness to work miracles in my life.*

MAY 1

But ignoring what they said, Jesus said
to the ruler of the synagogue, "Do not
fear, only believe." (Mark 5:36)

We are fortunate that the Bible contains many quotes coming directly from the mouth of Jesus. Reading his words can draw us closer to him and enhance our faith. Sometimes, however, his actions are just as powerful as his words.

As you attempt to grow in faith, you will encounter individuals who claim that you are being unrealistic. They will scoff at your belief in God's power to do all things and remind you that some situations are "hopeless." In his public ministry Jesus also encountered his share of naysayers. When the ruler of a synagogue asked Jesus to heal his daughter, the crowd laughed and proclaimed the girl already dead. Jesus *ignored them* and proceeded to raise her from the dead. If people try to convince you that you are being unrealistic by placing your faith in God, follow the example of Jesus and ignore them. They are the ones who are being unrealistic!

Jesus, I believe you can do all things and that no
situation is ever hopeless. I can stop worrying!

MAY 2

"But that you may know that the Son of man has authority on earth to forgive sins"—he said to the man who was paralyzed—"I say to you, rise, take up your bed and go home." (Luke 5:24)

Nothing gets our attention like a miracle. Many conversions have resulted from God healing the sick or doing the impossible. As wonderful as these visible signs can be, however, there are many unseen miracles that go unnoticed every day.

Jesus understands that human beings often have difficulty with things unseen. Therefore he will sometimes perform miraculous healings and interventions that can be seen or heard. Focusing too much on these visible incidents, however, can cause us to miss many of the *ordinary* miracles that occur in our lives each day. Childbirth, mended relationships, unlikely conversions, and the transformation of bread and wine into the Body and Blood of Christ at Mass are all examples of miracles that are often ignored. Make an effort to be more aware of the miracles that occur in your life. Learning to recognize them will make every day a joyful experience.

Today, Jesus, show me the everyday, ordinary
miracles that occur in my life on a regular basis.

MAY 3

And leaping up he stood and walked and entered the temple with them, walking and leaping and praising God. (Acts 3:8)

Does this verse describe you when you wake up in the morning? Very few of us react in this manner when the alarm clock sounds, but we probably should. Even if we don't physically leap out of bed, we should be grateful that God has given us another day.

How can we correct this tendency to overlook the many blessings that God gives us? Here is a technique that works for me. Each day as I eat my breakfast, I open my notebook and write a note to Jesus. I thank him for the gift of a new day and for many of the other blessings in my life—my wife, children, car, house, food, running water, electricity, and so on. Despite the fact that I am not a naturally grateful person, I have learned to appreciate many things I previously took for granted. If you begin to list all of the blessings in your life, I suspect you'll be leaping and praising God in no time!

Dear Jesus, thank you for this new day! I love you!

MAY 4

When the wine failed, the mother of Jesus said to him, "They have no wine." (John 2:3)

One thing is certain when it comes to Jesus—there's no such thing as "too late." While it definitely takes some getting used to, understanding this concept can help us relax. Much to our dismay God will often let us get to the edge of the cliff before saving the day.

At the wedding in Cana, Mary didn't approach Jesus when the wine was running low. She went to him when it was gone. Even though Jesus had not yet performed a public miracle, Mary knew he could do so. Waiting until the wine was completely out made Christ's first miracle even more powerful. Turn to the Blessed Mother with the problems in your life, and let her bring them to her Son. When you begin to panic because time is running out, think about this story. She knows just when to act, and so does Jesus!

Mary, I give you my problems and worries.
I trust that you will bring them to Jesus and
that he will respond at the correct time.

MAY 5

We know that in everything God works for good with those who love him, who are called according to his purpose. (Romans 8:28)

Not only is this one of the most comforting messages contained in the Bible, it's also one of the most ignored. Remembering this concept when troubles arise can mean the difference between anxiety and peace. In one sentence St. Paul reminds us that anything that happens to us is a blessing from God.

It's easy to see God at work during the pleasant times, but recognizing him in the midst of trials and suffering takes practice. The best way to start is to accept small inconveniences without complaining and acknowledge they are coming from God. By taking baby steps and accepting these minor annoyances, you will eventually be able to accept anything God sends your way.

God, I know that you love me and would never
do anything to harm me. Today I will accept any
inconveniences with patience and gratitude.

MAY 6

"If it be so, our God whom we serve is able to deliver us from the burning fiery furnace; and he will deliver us out of your hand, O king." (Daniel 3:17)

The examples of faith contained in the Bible can be mind-boggling. Even the threat of torture or death wasn't enough to make some of these courageous individuals turn their backs on God. In the case of Shadrach, Meshach, and Abednego, they were given a choice by King Nebuchadnezzar: either worship his golden idol or be thrown into a burning furnace.

Because they worshipped the one true God, the three men were not about to worship a golden image. Furthermore, because of their faith, they were not afraid of any punishments inflicted on them by the king. Before they were cast into the fire, they professed their belief in God's ability to protect them. And that is exactly what he did. In a similar way, God can protect us from the many dangers and challenges we face every day . . . if we give him a chance.

Please protect me from any physical and spiritual dangers I will face today, God.

MAY 7

And when they saw him they were astonished; and his mother said to him, "Son, why have you treated us so? Behold, your father and I have been looking for you anxiously." (Luke 2:48)

It is totally understandable that Mary and Joseph would be anxious when they were unable to find Jesus after leaving Jerusalem. Almost every parent can relate to the sick feeling that accompanies this frightening situation. While we can learn an important lesson from Joseph and Mary's urgency in seeking Jesus, Mary's words also provide valuable insight.

Upon finding Jesus in the temple, Mary was obviously confused. She didn't understand why this incident had happened. Sometimes we forget that, just like us, Mary was often perplexed by the events happening in her life. As a result, she didn't hesitate to ask questions. If you are confused about something you are facing, follow Mary's example and ask God what he is trying to teach you. Being open to his teaching is essential if you wish to grow in faith.

Jesus, I desire to follow your will. Please reveal what you are trying to teach me this day, especially through the situations in my life that confuse me.

MAY 8

"Ask and it will be given you; seek
and you will find; knock and it will be
opened to you." (Matthew 7:7)

When I was in school, I was always reluctant to ask my teachers for help. I thought it was a sign of weakness and avoided it at all costs. As a result I spent many hours worrying and spinning my wheels. By the time I got to college, however, my attitude had changed and I learned to ask for assistance. It was one of the best moves I could have made, as I never encountered a professor who refused to help me.

Jesus means what he says: When we ask, we will receive. Fortunately he loves us too much to give us anything that will harm us, and we can rest assured that we will receive the best possible answer to our prayer. Whether it's exactly what we requested or something better is his decision to make. Let's continue to do our job and ask for what we think we need. At the same time we should let Jesus do his job and provide what we truly need.

*I bring you all my spiritual and material
needs, Jesus, and I trust that you will always
answer my prayers in the best way possible.*

MAY 9

"O God, whose might is over all, hear the voice of the despairing, and save us from the hand of evildoers. And save me from my fear!" (Esther 14:19)

Queen Esther knew what it felt like to be anxious. In fact she was "seized with deathly anxiety" (Esther 14:1). Even when confronted with paralyzing fear, however, she knew what to do when all looked hopeless and her people were faced with destruction. Queen Esther turned to God and asked for help.

What I like about this Bible verse is that in addition to asking God to save her people, the wise queen asked to be saved from her fear! That's something many of us often forget to do when we are in the midst of a crisis. It's something we need to do, however, because fear can stop us dead in our tracks. God wants to help us with our problems, but he also wants to help us overcome our fear. Don't forget to ask!

God, you know how concerned I am
about certain situations. Please help
me to overcome my fear today.

MAY 10

Whatever your task, work heartily, as serving the Lord and not men, knowing that from the Lord you will receive the inheritance as your reward; you are serving the Lord Christ. (Colossians 3:23–24)

Do you find life boring? Are you tired of the drudgery you face every day? Do you ever wish that you could do something exciting with your life? You are in luck! In this Bible passage St. Paul provides you with the answer you have been waiting for. The most exciting job imaginable is yours for the taking.

What could be more rewarding than working for God? Unfortunately very few people know it is even possible. Fewer still know it is possible today! As Christians, any work we do can be performed for God. In his eyes cleaning toilets and brain surgery are equal. Keep this in mind as you perform your duties today. You are serving God. It doesn't get more exciting than that!

Jesus, I will remember that I'm serving you in all that I do today, no matter how small the task.

MAY 11

But the Lord said to him, "Peace be to you;
do not fear, you shall not die." (Judges 6:23)

Like many of us, Gideon suffered from a confidence problem. As a result he was stunned when informed by an angel that he had been chosen to deliver the Israelites from the oppression of the Midianites. Instead of dismissing the angel's message, however, Gideon asked for proof that it was truly coming from God. After receiving a sign, the young man was given further assurance from God: Despite the odds being against him, Gideon would not die in carrying out his mission.

Sometimes it seems that God is asking us to do the impossible. An extended illness, financial disaster, or unexpected death can feel like too much to handle. But just as God protected Gideon, he will protect us. Although it may not always seem like it, we are never alone.

Thank you for protecting me, God. Help
me to face my challenges with confidence,
knowing that you are with me.

MAY 12

And they laughed at him. (Mark 5:40)

One would think that someone who performed miracles would get some respect. This verse illustrates that it was not always the case for Jesus. What is even more astonishing is that he had just healed a woman who had been hemorrhaging for twelve years right before the eyes of those who were laughing. They just couldn't accept it, however, when he claimed that the daughter of Jairus wasn't dead, but sleeping. And so they laughed.

We all will encounter those individuals who laugh when we express our faith in God. We shouldn't let it affect us. If people laughed at Jesus, why wouldn't they laugh at us? Our example of faith is exactly what they need to see.

Jesus, help me not to become discouraged
when people make fun of my faith in you.

MAY 13

And when they had prayed, the place in which they were gathered together was shaken; and they were all filled with the Holy Spirit and spoke the word of God with boldness. (Acts 4:31)

In my younger days it was not easy for me to share my faith. Fear of looking strange and a lack of knowledge caused me to clam up on many occasions when I should have spoken up. This is a common problem for many individuals, but it can be overcome. As this verse illustrates, we can all speak the Word of God with boldness when we learn to depend on the power of the Holy Spirit.

Knowing that we should speak up but not knowing what to say can cause a great deal of anxiety. Fortunately the Holy Spirit can help us. Even if we don't say the "perfect" words, the Spirit can enable the listener to hear what he or she is supposed to hear. As can be seen in this Bible verse, it all begins with prayer. Turn to the Holy Spirit and you will not be disappointed.

Holy Spirit, I am often overcome with a lack of confidence when it comes to talking about my faith. Help me to remember you, especially when I engage in a difficult conversation.

MAY 14

"But take heed to yourselves lest your hearts be weighed down with dissipation and drunkenness and cares of this life, and that day come upon you suddenly like a snare." (Luke 21:34)

If we are not careful, we can become so distracted by the cares and pleasures of life that we lose sight of the big picture. We were created by God to live with him forever in heaven. Our life on earth gives us the opportunity to know, love, and serve him, but it is temporary. Remembering this will not only reduce much of your stress, it will ensure that you reach your final destination.

Every problem you will face in this life is temporary. Some last longer than others, but they will all disappear when you die. If you spend an excessive amount of time worrying about these passing struggles, you'll waste valuable time that could be spent speaking to God and enjoying his presence.

God, when my heart feels weighed down by the cares and concerns of this life, let it serve as a reminder to stay focused on you and the promise of eternal life. May I spend all of my days knowing, loving, and serving you.

MAY 15

When I am afraid, I put my trust
in you. (Psalm 56:3)

Do you know what I like about this verse? It reminds me that
it is perfectly acceptable to be afraid. Fear is simply an emotion—one that can be very useful in alerting us to potential
danger. It can even lead us closer to God as we run to him
for protection. As long as we do that, we're in good shape.

I have a long history of responding to fear with worry
and useless imaginings. Instead of running into the arms
of my loving Father, I have frequently run away from him.
When we are afraid, we should immediately turn to God.
The fact that we still feel nervous doesn't matter as long as
we're praying. If you are an anxious person and put this into
practice frequently, you will grow very close to God. You
may even begin to feel, as I do, that anxiety can be a blessing.

When I am afraid, Jesus, I will choose to
turn my back on fear and trust in you.

MAY 16

For you know the grace of our Lord Jesus Christ, that though he was rich, yet for your sake he became poor, so that by his poverty you might become rich. (2 Corinthians 8:9)

Doing God's will is not always pleasant. No matter how close we are to him, there will be certain things in life we would rather avoid. Learning to rise above our feelings and do what God wants is how we become holy.

When Jesus became man he willingly subjected himself to all the pain that goes along with being human. He experienced tiredness, hunger, and humiliation from his enemies. He even experienced death. Why? Because he loves us. By accepting the suffering that comes our way, you and I have a chance to express our love for him. On the other hand, we can choose to complain about the weather, our health, our tiredness, and many other things, but what good does that do?

Jesus, I offer up any unpleasant situations I encounter today. Thank you for allowing me to express my love for you by accepting everything from your hand.

MAY 17

And the king said to her, "Make your request, my mother; for I will not refuse you." (1 Kings 2:20)

When Adonijah needed a favor from King Solomon, he first approached the king's mother and informed her of his need. Bathsheba then presented the request to her son, the king. Even before learning the details, Solomon promised that he would grant his mother's wish. Why is this story important to us? It's significant because it foreshadows the intercessory power of the Blessed Mother.

At the wedding in Cana (see John 2:1–11), we see an example of what happens when Mary approaches her Son to request a favor. Just like Solomon, he will not refuse his mother. In this month dedicated to Our Lady, make it a point to turn to her frequently. Knowing that she will be hand-delivering your intentions to her Son should definitely increase your confidence!

Blessed Mother, please bring my intentions to Jesus. Thank you for interceding on my behalf.

MAY 18

Draw near to God and he will
draw near to you. (James 4:8)

It's been said that God works in mysterious ways. Many of his actions leave us scratching our heads and wondering what he is up to. Something that has always perplexed me is God's refusal to force his way into our lives. Even though he knows that we need him, he waits for us to open the door and invite him inside.

One thing you can count on is that God will never reject your efforts to grow closer to him. Whenever you make an attempt to draw near, he will respond. Don't let the challenges of life distract you. Get into the habit of inviting him into your life every day. It is definitely worth the effort!

*God, I invite you into my life, and I ask
that you draw me closer to you today.*

MAY 19

Do you not know that you are God's temple and that God's Spirit dwells in you? (1 Corinthians 3:16)

Several years ago I worked as a software developer and was heavily involved in a major transition. All of our antiquated computer hardware was replaced with brand-new equipment, and we were faced with a huge learning curve. In order to help us, management hired an individual who was familiar with the new technology. For several months he worked side by side with us until we were comfortable with the new machinery.

Our fallen human nature makes it difficult for us to do the right thing. As a result God sends the Holy Spirit to help us to rise above our sinful inclinations. God's Spirit is not helping you from a distance—he is actually dwelling inside you! With his help no situation is too challenging for you to handle. Learn to depend on him as you face the struggles of daily life.

Thank you for dwelling in me, Holy Spirit.
Inspire me to know what to do and how to act.

MAY 20

And this is the testimony, that God gave us
eternal life, and this life is in his Son. (1 John 5:11)

Before I make a major purchase, I always like to do some
research. Online product reviews can be very useful in helping me decide which model or brand to choose. Even a less
important decision, such as trying a new restaurant, can be
simplified by speaking to individuals who have eaten there.
Seeking the testimony of others is a very wise and common
practice.

St. John states that the testimony of God is greater than
that of men (see 1 John 5:9). And God testifies that eternal
life is possible through Jesus Christ. No matter what kind of
problems you are facing, you should be uplifted by this fact.
Now is the time to get to know Jesus personally. If eternal
life in heaven is possible only through Christ, shouldn't we
make it a priority to get to know him better?

Jesus, thank you for making eternal life
in heaven a possibility. Increase my desire
to know you better here on earth.

MAY 21

"Be strong and of good courage, do not
fear or be in dread of them: for it is the Lord
your God who goes with you; he will not fail
you or forsake you." (Deuteronomy 31:6)

Just prior to speaking these words to the Israelites, Moses
informed them that he would not be leading them into
the Promised Land. More importantly he assured them
that God would be with them on the journey. Even though
Joshua would lead them across the Jordan River, God was
ultimately in charge and would protect them from their
enemies.

Because he is invisible we can easily forget about God's
constant presence in our life. As we struggle to deal with
problems and challenges, we might feel that everything depends on us. It doesn't. God is always with us. Remembering
that simple fact can spare us much aggravation!

God, sometimes it seems like everything
depends on me, and I feel overwhelmed.
Today I choose to let go of that false sense of
control and be courageous in you instead.

MAY 22

But do not ignore this one fact, beloved, that with the Lord one day is as a thousand years, and a thousand years as one day. (2 Peter 3:8)

Ever have one of those jobs in which the minutes pass like hours? How about a vacation in which the days seem to fly by? For completely different reasons each of these situations can be very frustrating. Depending on the circumstances we can view the passage of time as our friend or our enemy.

Much of our frustration about time is due to impatience. We live in a world that has become accustomed to instant gratification. Whether we're talking about food or Internet speed, we don't like to wait. God, on the other hand, is not impatient. He will give us what we need when the time is right. Keep this in mind as you continue to pray for something you needed "yesterday." God really does know what he's doing.

God, your timing is always perfect. Teach me to be patient and not expect instant answers.

MAY 23

And they worshiped him, and returned to
Jerusalem with great joy, and were continually
in the temple blessing God. (Luke 24:52–53)

With these words the Gospel of St. Luke draws to a close.
Looking carefully at this passage gives us a good idea of how
the apostles felt after Jesus ascended into heaven. When I
read it, three words jump out at me: *with great joy*. They
express what a relationship with Jesus can do in our lives.

Just before ascending into heaven, Jesus commissioned
the twelve to continue his work of spreading the Good News.
They would be doing this in a world filled with hostility toward Christ and his followers. They would also be working
without the luxury of having Jesus in their midst. Why, then,
would they possess "great joy"? This is the result of having
a personal relationship with Jesus Christ. He is the ultimate
source of joy, and walking with him each day will unleash
that joy in our lives.

Jesus, I long to experience the daily joy
that flows from being close to you.

MAY 24

Again Jesus spoke to them, saying,
"I am the light of the world; he who
follows me will not walk in darkness, but
will have the light of life." (John 8:12)

The Pharisees reacted to these words in exactly the way we might have expected. They told Jesus that they didn't believe him. And while it's easy for us to criticize them, we often do the same thing. We may not make an explicit proclamation, but our actions speak louder than words.

When we ignore the words of Christ, we are choosing to walk in the darkness. As a result we end up lacking peace and overcomplicating our lives. Just like the Pharisees, we can lose sight of the big picture and end up becoming self-righteous. Before we know it we are walking in the dark needlessly. Following Jesus faithfully is the only way to guarantee that we will remain in the light.

*Thank you for your guidance, Jesus. I am grateful
that you continue to illuminate my path.*

MAY 25

Cast your burden on the Lord, and he will sustain you; he will never permit the righteous to be moved. (Psalm 55:22)

I like to fix problems. While generally a good thing, this tendency can sometimes cause additional problems, especially when I'm trying to help others. There are times when the best thing I can do is to listen. At one time or another, everyone needs a shoulder to cry on. Providing that shoulder can bring great comfort to someone who is hurting.

As helpful as I can be as a listener, there is someone who far exceeds my ability. He has the broadest shoulders imaginable and is always willing to listen to our problems. Don't be afraid to vent to Jesus. Let him know all your concerns and complaints. While you should also mix in some prayers of thanksgiving, God loves you and wants you to share everything with him. Give it a try today. I guarantee you'll feel better.

Your unconditional love amazes me, Jesus. Thank you for being so interested in my problems, no matter how small. You are a true friend!

MAY 26

Now faith is the assurance of things hoped for, the conviction of things not seen. (Hebrews 11:1)

I tend to be a bit skeptical at times, even when I receive the assurance of others. Throughout my life I have been assured of many things that didn't work out as promised, and it has affected the way I think. While being cautious can be helpful, it can also be a hindrance—especially when it comes to faith.

Having faith in God requires believing some rather unbelievable promises. Faith is a gift, and it enables us to believe that God speaks the truth. Unlike many individuals who provide us with empty assurances, God's promises are always true; the gift of faith makes it possible to believe in them. Unfortunately many individuals waste this great gift by not using it. Don't make that mistake. Make it a point to use your faith today!

I am grateful for the gift of faith, Jesus. I will make an effort to use it throughout the day to believe in your promises.

MAY 27

And Sarai said to Abram, "Behold now, the Lord has prevented me from bearing children; go in to my maid; it may be that I obtain children by her." And Abram listened to the voice of Sarai. (Genesis 16:2)

Believing in God's promise that they would have children must have been difficult for Abram and Sarai (a.k.a. Abraham and Sarah), especially as they approached the century mark. In all fairness it's easy to see why they thought they were missing something. Taking matters into her own hands, Sarai suggested to Abram that he try having children with her maid.

Even though Abram agreed (and ended up fathering a son with Sarai's maid), this wasn't what God had in mind when he promised the couple numerous descendants. Defying the odds, Sarai eventually became pregnant, and God's promise was fulfilled. There are two important lessons from this story. First, all things are possible with God. Second, God can always bring good out of any mistake that we make. Be confident that he is with you today.

Help me to trust you with my life, God. I know that you can bring good out of any mistake I make.

MAY 28

So he went down and dipped himself seven times in the Jordan, according to the word of the man of God; and his flesh was restored like the flesh of a little child, and he was clean. (2 Kings 5:14)

Naaman, a Syrian commander, was a man of great power. He was also afflicted with leprosy and sought to be cured. Upon visiting Elisha the prophet, Naaman was told to wash in the Jordan seven times. He became angry at the instructions from the prophet, believing that the cure should come about in another way. Eventually his servants convinced him to obey Elisha's command—and he was cured.

Before we criticize Naaman, how many times have we acted in a similar way? We pursue miraculous healings or supernatural messages while ignoring the infinite power contained in the sacraments. Familiar prayers such as the Our Father and the Hail Mary can be overlooked and considered too simplistic. As Naaman discovered, God's miracles can often look rather ordinary. Forgetting this would be a big mistake.

God, help me to recognize your great power
at all times, even when it seems ordinary.

MAY 29

"For where your treasure is, there will your heart be also." (Luke 12:34)

One can learn a great deal about a person by looking at his or her possessions. We tend to pursue those things in life that are important to us. Even a *lack* of material possessions can reveal much about an individual. Jesus understood this very well, as this popular Bible verse illustrates.

It may be spiritual or it may be material, but we all have something that is important to us. What is your treasure? Take some time to reflect on this question today. You can ask the Holy Spirit to help you. While there is nothing wrong with having possessions, there is something wrong with letting them possess you.

Jesus, I know that you are the greatest treasure anyone could ever have. Please show me anything in my life that I value more than you and give me the grace to let it go.

MAY 30

Trust in the Lord for ever, for the Lord
God is an everlasting rock. (Isaiah 26:4)

The expression "solid as a rock" is certainly an accurate one.
When we think of a rock, we don't typically picture something flimsy or temporary. If you've ever encountered one
while digging in your garden, you know exactly what I mean.
In describing God as an "everlasting rock," the prophet Isaiah gives us a strong mental image of someone who is unchanging and almighty.

In a world filled with change, the stability of God is
comforting. When faced with unexpected challenges, we can
take refuge in him. Take a look around you and recognize
that everything you see is temporary. Then pause and remember that God has always existed and will never cease to
be. That's why Isaiah referred to him as a rock!

*Glory be to the Father and to the Son and to the
Holy Spirit. As it was in the beginning, is now,
and ever shall be, world without end. Amen.*

MAY 31

For God has not destined us for wrath,
but to obtain salvation through our Lord
Jesus Christ. (1 Thessalonians 5:9)

Would you like some good news today? You were created to live with God forever in heaven. Even though you may have to suffer in this life, there is something great waiting for you after you die. Many times, though, the problems and worries you face each day can cause you to lose sight of the big picture.

Make no mistake about it, looking beyond the drudgery and pain of daily life requires work. It doesn't just happen by itself. In order to appreciate God's generosity, it is a good idea to think about where you would be without him. Jesus Christ gave his life so that your salvation would be possible. All the pain and mental anguish that he suffered was an expression of his love for you. He spent three hours hanging on a cross so you could experience eternal happiness in heaven. Can you spare a few minutes each day thinking about that?

When I think about what you suffered for
me, I am very grateful for your generosity.
Keep me focused on the big picture.

JUNE 1

And he said to them, "Why are you afraid,
O men of little faith?" Then he rose and
rebuked the winds and the sea; and there
was a great calm. (Matthew 8:26)

Before calming the storm at sea, Jesus made sure he took advantage of a great teaching moment. By doing so he not only instructed his disciples but also sent a message to us. If our faith is strong, is there ever a reason to panic? Sure, there are times when we should be concerned, but panicking indicates a lack of trust in God's providence.

Just like the disciples, we all tend to panic at times. Rather than accepting it, however, we should view this as an issue that needs to be addressed. Look back on your life and recognize the many times God brought you through difficult situations. Thank him and ask him for a greater trust in his providence. Although it is a process and does require time, you should gradually find yourself panicking less and trusting more.

*Thank you for rescuing me so many
times, Jesus. When I'm tempted to
panic, fill me with trust in you.*

JUNE 2

For the foolishness of God is wiser than men, and the weakness of God is stronger than men. (1 Corinthians 1:25)

Foolishness? Weakness? By using anthropomorphism (a literary technique that assigns human qualities to God), St. Paul definitely grabbed the attention of his readers. Don't think for a minute that Paul believed God could ever exhibit either of these qualities. Instead he used some shocking words to make an important point: God is wiser and stronger than we are!

Why is it important to state the obvious? Does anybody truly believe they know more than God? Not only does it happen all the time, but we are the ones who do it! When unpleasant things happen, we often lash out at God. When our prayers aren't answered quickly enough, we get annoyed and begin to doubt. Instead of constantly criticizing God's actions, we should spend time reflecting on his wisdom and power. Doing so will give us a greater desire to place our lives in his hands.

I praise you for your infinite strength and wisdom, God. Thank you for continuing to provide for all my needs.

JUNE 3

"And you will be hated by all for my name's sake. But he who endures to the end will be saved." (Mark 13:13)

It's difficult to understand why anyone would reject a message of love and hope. But that is exactly what happened when Jesus preached it two thousand years ago, and it still happens today. Anyone who tries to spread the Good News eventually discovers what it's like to be rejected—or even hated.

Jesus knew what we would face, and he wants us to be prepared. He also wants us to know that there is a light at the end of the tunnel. No matter what kind of opposition or hatred we encounter, there is a reward waiting for us if we continue to share his message with others. Keep your eye on the prize—it will all be worth it in the end.

Dear Jesus, please grant me the strength to
continue sharing your message with others.

JUNE 4

For by grace you have been saved through faith; and this is not your own doing, it is the gift of God. (Ephesians 2:8)

Entitlement can be a dangerous attitude, especially when it comes to spiritual matters. Believing that I have a right to live forever in heaven because I am a good person actually jeopardizes my chances of getting there. In a similar way, failing to recognize God's generosity (especially when it comes to grace) is a huge mistake.

While it is true that we were all created to live with God in heaven, we need help to get there. Our eternal happiness is possible only through the sacrifice of Jesus Christ and the graces that flow through his Church. The fact that we need his help shouldn't make us feel sad—it should fill us with gratitude. Take some time today to reflect on the great future that is planned for you. No matter how many struggles you will face in your lifetime, one thing will never change: You were created for heaven!

Thank you for making it possible for me to live with you in heaven, Lord. When I think of the great future that stretches for all eternity, it changes the way I view my daily life.

JUNE 5

So Abram went, as the Lord had told him; and Lot went with him. Abram was seventy-five years old when he departed from Haran. (Genesis 12:4)

Congratulations! You have been given the gift of another day. Even though you may not realize it, God has a mission for you. It is a special task that only you can complete. And as illustrated by the calling of Abram at the age of seventy-five, it's never too late for God to put you to work.

With each new day we have the opportunity to do something for God. There are no exceptions. If you are alive, you can serve God in some way. It may involve physical activity or it may simply consist of praying or offering up your suffering. Ask God what you can do for him today. No matter how many days or years you have wasted, it's never too late to get started. Today is a new beginning!

God, thank you for giving me another day and
a new beginning. Show me how I can serve
you today as I go about my daily tasks.

JUNE 6

And Jesus said to him, "If you can! All things are possible to him who believes." (Mark 9:23)

The Power of Positive Thinking by Norman Vincent Peale is a classic book that has helped many individuals to discover the benefits of optimism. While I definitely believe his concept has merit, I feel equally strongly about the power of *negative* thinking. Why? Because by failing to believe in God's power, you can actually block him from working miracles in your life.

Obviously blocking the power of God is not something we want to do, but it happens frequently. You run the risk of doing so every time you fail to pray for a "hopeless" situation in your life. Unless you ask you will never know what miracles Jesus has in store for you. Think of the seemingly hopeless situations in your life and ask God to resolve them. It may require patience, but keep asking. I guarantee that by doing this consistently, you will discover that many of these problems aren't hopeless after all.

God, show me the places where I block your power in my life. I trust that you have miracles in store for me!

JUNE 7

For everything there is a season, and a time for every matter under heaven. (Ecclesiastes 3:1)

When our daughters were born three months premature, Eileen and I accepted the fact that they would be spending several months in the hospital. During these challenging months a piece of advice given to us by one of the nurses was extremely helpful. Preparing us for what was to come, she cautioned us not to get too excited about the good days or too upset about the bad days. It proved to be wise advice and helped us to get through a difficult period in our life.

The Book of Ecclesiastes has a similar message: Life is a series of ups and downs. Over the course of our lives, we will experience a mixture of suffering and joy, a kaleidoscope of highs and lows. It's important to remember that everything in this life is temporary. Learning to roll with the punches and enjoy the constant support of God will bring us a great deal of peace and keep us balanced.

I know that you are always there for me, God, in good times and bad. Grant me the grace to endure all the seasons of my life with courage and confidence.

JUNE 8

Have no anxiety about anything, but in everything by prayer and supplication with thanksgiving let your requests be made known to God. (Philippians 4:6)

If you are a chronic worrier, it is just about impossible to force yourself to stop worrying. On the other hand, it is totally possible to break free from worrying. How? This Bible verse provides the answer. St. Paul recommends that instead of wasting your time worrying about the difficulties in your life, you turn to Jesus in prayer.

This simple advice has made a huge difference in my life. Although I still have a tendency to be anxious, I have learned to bring my concerns to God. The mere act of turning to him in prayer generally brings an increased sense of peace. I've also learned to follow Paul's advice and include thanksgiving in my prayer. No matter how worrisome life seems to be, we can always be thankful for something. The fact that God is always listening and willing to help us is a good place to start.

Thank you for your willingness to listen to me, God. I give you what is causing me to worry today, thankful that you offer me your peace in return.

JUNE 9

"Lord, I am ready to go with you to prison and to death." (Luke 22:33)

Have you ever broken a promise you made to God? I know I have. It can be a very discouraging experience. It can even plunge you into despair and cause you to think you are hopeless. That is exactly what the evil one wants you to think—and it's a lie. What it really means is that, just like St. Peter, you are human!

Peter's heart was certainly in the right place, but he obviously didn't realize what he was up against. Having a fallen human nature (like the rest of us), he wasn't able to follow through on his promise. However, there's more to the story. Even though Peter failed in a big way, Jesus gave him another chance. That same mercy extends to each of us. If you have sinned, consider it a reminder that you need God's assistance. Seek his forgiveness (the sacrament of reconciliation is perfect for this) and ask for the grace to do better next time. If it worked for St. Peter, it will work for you.

I know you will never give up on me, God. No matter how many times I fall, you've promised to always forgive me. Thank you for the gift of confession.

JUNE 10

For even if we sin we are yours, knowing your power; but we will not sin, because we know that we are considered yours. (Wisdom 15:2)

I didn't get into too much trouble when I was a child, but I had my moments. Fortunately the blessing of a guilty conscience kept me from getting into big trouble. I loved my parents and never wanted to disappoint them. When I would occasionally follow my desires and engage in activities that were not exactly wholesome, I would experience so much guilt that I would quickly confess to my parents and face the consequences.

Our heavenly Father loves us unconditionally. His love does not change even when we fall into sin. If we truly love him, however, it makes sense for us to do whatever we can to avoid displeasing him. Instead of becoming discouraged with your inability to do the right thing, make an effort to become better acquainted with Jesus. Eventually the desire to please him will outweigh the attractiveness of sin.

Jesus, I want to have a deeply personal relationship with you, and I know that it is possible. Today I choose to turn away from sin and grow closer to you.

JUNE 11

Now you are the body of Christ and individually members of it. (1 Corinthians 12:27)

How does it make you feel to know that you are part of the body of Christ? While most people don't think about it, baptism connects us with God in an extremely intimate way. Although the concept can be abstract and difficult to understand, it is worth exploring. Even a surface understanding will help you to realize that you are an important part of a very special family.

As part of the mystical body of Christ, you are never alone. No matter what difficulties you face in life, you have a heavenly Father to assist you and the Holy Spirit to guide you. Furthermore, you have Jesus in your life. He loves you so much that he doesn't settle for just being beside you. As difficult as it can be to understand, you are actually a part of him. Now that's what I call a close friend!

*Dear Jesus, thank you for letting me be
a part of your mystical body. Help me to
better appreciate this amazing gift.*

JUNE 12

And Jesus looking upon him loved him, and said
to him, "You lack one thing; go, sell what you have,
and give to the poor, and you will have treasure
in heaven; and come, follow me." (Mark 10:21)

There is something appealing about the idea of instant gratification. For many individuals, dipping into the french fries while driving home from a fast-food restaurant is a regular practice. In general we don't like to wait to experience pleasure. We want it now!

Jesus' command to the rich young man was not well received. The promise of treasure in heaven wasn't as appealing as the comfort obtained from his possessions. The young man made a big mistake, though. Everything in this life is temporary, and the pleasure associated with earthly treasures will fade. The treasure awaiting us in heaven will last forever, and that's definitely worth the wait.

I know that great joy awaits me in heaven,
Jesus. Help me to be patient and focus on
doing what is necessary to get there.

JUNE 13

Wisdom and knowledge are granted to you. I will also give you riches, possessions, and honor, such as none of the kings had who were before you, and none after you shall have the like. (2 Chronicles 1:12)

Imagine the joy that you would feel if God appeared to you and asked, "What would you like me to give you?" How would you answer that question? For King Solomon this hypothetical encounter actually happened—and his answer may surprise you. Instead of material possessions or power, the king asked for wisdom so he could govern the people justly.

God not only granted Solomon's request, he also provided him with riches, possessions, and honor. There is an important lesson contained in this story. The Lord knows we have material needs, but sometimes our spiritual needs are more important. It's possible that without first having wisdom, Solomon would have abused riches, possessions, and honor. Make it a point to ask God for the spiritual treasures that you lack. You may be surprised with the other gifts he gives you as well.

Jesus, open my eyes to the spiritual gifts you've blessed me with, and help me to see these are far more important than any material things I am longing for.

JUNE 14

"I am the living bread which came down from heaven; if any one eats of this bread, he will live for ever; and the bread which I shall give for the life of the world is my flesh." (John 6:51)

When these words were first spoken by Jesus two thousand years ago, they were shocking. The Eucharist had not yet been instituted, and Jesus' apparent endorsement of cannibalism caused many of his followers to desert him (see John 6:66). As Catholics looking at this verse in the twenty-first century, we are no longer shocked by the words of Jesus. While that is a positive development, there is a downside to our acceptance of these words. We may have become so familiar with the his message that it fails to excite us. That is a shame.

In the Eucharist we have a great gift—Jesus' presence in a real and mysterious way. Receiving the Eucharist daily has changed my life, and it can change yours as well. Making the effort to attend one or two daily Masses each week (in addition to Sunday) can have a huge impact on your life. Try it out and see what happens.

Jesus, thank you that I can receive you in
Holy Communion. It is a great gift!

JUNE 15

"So take heart, men, for I have faith in God that it will be exactly as I have been told." (Acts 27:25)

It can be very difficult to trust God in the midst of a raging storm. But because of his great faith, that is exactly what St. Paul was able to do. As he sailed to Rome in a ship battered by a powerful storm, Paul was assured by an angel that everyone on board would survive. He then proceeded to relay the message to the crew.

In order for us to share the message of hope with those around us, we first need to believe it ourselves. Do you believe that God can bring good out of any situation that happens in your life (see Romans 8:28)? Do you believe that he will never give you more than you can handle (see 1 Corinthians 10:13)? Do you believe that with his help you can do anything (Philippians 4:13)? If you're not quite there, ask St. Paul to intercede for you. He truly believed in God's trustworthiness, and with a little help, you can, too.

St. Paul, I would like to trust God as much
as you did. Please pray for me!

JUNE 16

The Lord is my shepherd,
I shall not want. (Psalm 23:1)

If you struggle with anxiety, there is a good chance that you are familiar with Psalm 23. It has been bringing comfort to worriers for thousands of years. Slowly reading and reflecting on the words of this psalm has brought me peace time and time again. And while I do recommend reading all of the verses, the first verse sums up the overall message in a succinct way: If I have God in my life, I have all that I need.

If this is true, why do we have so many unsatisfied wants? Often it is because we are confusing our wants with our needs. Life is filled with distractions, and we can easily lose sight of the fact that God can satisfy all of our needs. As we grow closer to him, we might realize that many of our wants aren't really that important after all. If you have God in your life, you have all you need.

God, thank you for fulfilling all my needs.
If I have you, I have everything!

JUNE 17

Do not love the world or the things in the world. If any one loves the world, love for the Father is not in him. (1 John 2:15)

No doubt about it, this is a tough message. Many individuals look at the words of St. John and reject them as being too harsh. After all, didn't God create the world? What could be wrong with loving his creation?

This message is all about desire. If my ultimate goal in life is to serve God, I am in good shape. On the other hand, pursuing riches and fame in order to live a life of comfort is problematic. While there is nothing sinful about earning a good living, it should never be more important than your relationship with God. Lasting peace can be found in him alone.

Father, speak to my heart and help me to
love you above all. Please remove anything
that gets in the way of our relationship.

JUNE 18

"Be still, and know that I am God."
(Psalm 46:10)

Most worry-prone individuals like to be in control. This often results in an excessive desire to be busy and get things done. For this type of individual, the thought of being still can be a painful one. In today's noisy and extremely busy world, however, it is the best way to encounter God—just as it was in the psalmist's day.

In the past I would only pray when I felt like it or when I wasn't busy. Now I choose to spend some quiet time with Jesus every day, no matter what. Even though it can be extremely difficult to sit still when e-mails have to be answered and writing deadlines met, I choose to do it anyway. Through this act of self-discipline, my relationship with him has grown, and I can feel his presence in my life more deeply. I know the frustration that comes from running around and trying to control every area of my life, and I also know the peace that comes from spending quiet time in the God's presence. In the end can you guess which is more worthwhile?

Jesus, grant me the discipline to spend some quiet time with you each day, no matter how busy my life might be.

JUNE 19

No distrust made him waver concerning the promise of God, but he grew strong in his faith as he gave glory to God, fully convinced that God was able to do what he had promised. (Romans 5:20–21)

How do you react when God is slow to answer your prayers? Do you respond by dwelling on his failure to answer, or do you offer praise for his great power? Although it seems counterintuitive, Abraham chose the latter option. As a result his faith grew by leaps and bounds. Despite his advanced age he remained fully convinced that God would somehow find a way to grant him descendants.

When faced with unanswered prayers, one of the best things you can do is praise God. Acknowledging his power and greatness will give you the assurance that he can do what he promised. God can do all things, but you need to believe it or else you will eventually stop praying. No matter how miserable or discouraged you feel, spend some time praising God for his omnipotence. He truly can do all things. Keep reminding yourself of it!

Glory to you, Lord Jesus Christ. You are all-powerful—
let me never forget that you can do anything!

JUNE 20

The Lord said to Gideon, "The people with you are too many to give the Midianites into their hand, lest Israel vaunt themselves against me, saying, 'My own hand has delivered me.'" (Judges 7:2)

God knows us better than we know ourselves. He understands our tendency to take credit for the great things he accomplishes in our lives. If not corrected this can lead to a false sense of self-sufficiency. Once that happens we are only a few steps away from distancing ourselves from him and ceasing to pray.

Because he is all-loving, God often reminds us that we need him. If you are discouraged because you've committed the same sin for the millionth time or you've done poorly on a job interview that you thought was a sure thing, let it serve as a reminder of just how much you need God's help. Let your weaknesses and defeats lead you to the loving arms of your heavenly Father. With his help you *can* do all things!

I need you, Jesus. Without you I can do nothing—but with you I can do all things!

JUNE 21

Can a man hide himself in secret places so that I cannot see him? says the Lord. Do I not fill heaven and earth? says the Lord. (Jeremiah 23:24)

Isn't it great to know that God is watching over you? No matter where you go or what you do, he sees you. While this is a comforting thought, there is a bigger picture we often fail to see. Sometimes we may picture God sitting in heaven, viewing our lives on a video monitor. In reality, though, he is much closer than that.

Losing sight of God's presence is a big mistake. He does not watch over us from a distance by using a webcam; instead he is right beside us. He is everywhere we go. This implies that no matter how lonely and frightened you may feel, you are never truly alone. Keep that in mind the next time you face a frightening situation. Jesus is right there with you. Don't forget to speak to him!

Thank you for being with me wherever I go, Jesus. You are a true friend, and your presence is such a gift!

JUNE 22

But even if you do suffer for righteousness'
sake, you will be blessed. Have no fear of
them or be troubled, but in your hearts
reverence Christ as Lord. (1 Peter 3:14–15)

If you tell others about your faith, if you share the Good News of Jesus Christ, expect to be persecuted. Even if it doesn't result in physical harm, sharing the gospel often results in verbal abuse. Fear of rejection can cause you to cease your evangelization efforts. But as St. Peter asserts in this passage, temporary discomfort results in permanent blessings.

Christ warned us that we would be hated because of him, but he also promised that the righteous would be blessed. It's challenging to hold on to his promise when we experience persecution, but don't let the momentary pain of rejection or humiliation stop you. Jesus wants you to share his message with a world that desperately needs to hear it, whether it accepts it or not.

Jesus, I know I will experience persecution for
sharing your message. Please grant me the strength
to get out of my comfort zone and persevere.

JUNE 23

And he said to his disciples, "Therefore I
tell you, do not be anxious about your life,
what you shall eat, nor about your body,
what you shall put on." (Luke 12:22)

There is a big difference between being anxious and being responsible. While Jesus fully expects us to use our talents and intellect to provide for our material needs, he doesn't want us to worry about the future. Even though it can be extremely difficult, he wants us to trust him with our lives. One of the best ways to get started with this is to take life one day at a time.

Rather than worrying about an endless stream of what-ifs, we should learn to deal with the problems that exist today. After doing what we can to solve our issues, we can step back and let God do his thing. This may take some self-discipline, but it absolutely will be worth it in the end. God has a long history of providing for the needs of his people. Don't think for a minute that you will be the first exception!

The future can be very frightening for me,
God. Today I give you all my what-ifs, trusting
that you will provide for my needs.

JUNE 24

"He must increase, but I must decrease." (John 3:30)

St. John the Baptist certainly understood his role. Even though he attracted a great deal of attention, he knew his primary job was to bring people closer to Jesus. Once Jesus began his public ministry, John realized it was time to get out of the way. Putting this concept into practice in our own lives can bear great fruit.

There is so much misery in the world. Many individuals are sleepwalking through life, not knowing the peace that comes from a relationship with Jesus Christ. By letting God work through us as St. John did, we can share Jesus with others. Doing so will bring greater peace not only to them, but to us as well.

St. John the Baptist, pray for us.

JUNE 25

"Who is like you, O Lord, among the gods? Who is like you, majestic in holiness, terrible in glorious deeds, doing wonders?" (Exodus 15:11)

Having survived the life-threatening pursuit of the Egyptians, Moses led his people in a song of praise. His words acknowledged the power of almighty God, whose miraculous intervention saved the Israelites from certain death. Moses also brings up a very good point: Is there anyone as powerful as God?

Just like Moses, we know the answer to this question . . . or do we? Every time we worry about the future or lose sleep over an ongoing problem, we fail to recognize God's infinite power. Why would we worry if we thought he could do all things? Let's spend some time today thinking about what God did for the Israelites and what he has done for us. It will help us to realize just how powerful he is.

You are all-powerful, God. Thank you for the many miracles you have performed through the ages—and in my own life, too!

JUNE 26

For he satisfies him who is thirsty, and the
hungry he fills with good things. (Psalm 107:9)

If you are reading this book, it is highly likely that you are
seeking peace. There is also a very good chance that you
understand God's ability to fulfill that desire. Sadly many
people don't realize that the only lasting peace comes from
having a personal relationship with Jesus Christ. Through
him, and only through him, can we experience a deep peace
that doesn't depend on external circumstances.

For many years I sought peace through the things of the
world. Despite my best efforts I remained miserable. It was
only when I turned to God that my desires were granted. I
experienced the peace I wanted so desperately. If you hunger
and thirst for a deep and lasting peace, look to Jesus. He will
satisfy your desires.

*Jesus, no matter what problems I'm facing these
days, I know only you can satisfy my desire for peace.
Thank you for filling my life with good things.*

JUNE 27

He considered that God was able to raise men even from the dead. (Hebrews 11:19)

Have you ever wondered how Abraham was able to go along with God's request to sacrifice his son Isaac? This verse provides the answer. As astonishing as it may seem, Abraham's faith was so strong that he believed in God's ability to do anything—including raising the dead.

What are your expectations when you pray? Do you anticipate miraculous results? In all honesty most of us are lacking in the faith department and could use some of what Abraham had. One of the best ways to grow in faith is to ask God for big things. Not frivolous, but big. Give him the chance to work miracles in your life and see what happens. Never underestimate what God can do!

Give me the kind of faith Abraham had, Father.
From this point on I will stop underestimating
you and give you the chance to do great things
in my life. No problem is too big for you!

JUNE 28

On the following day, when they came from
Bethany, he was hungry. (Mark 11:12)

I still have a tendency to worry. If you have read my books
or heard me speak on television or radio, this probably does
not come as a surprise to you. Because of my experience as
a worrier, people know that I understand what it feels like
to be anxious. As a result my message is believable to them.

Jesus had a human (as well as a divine) nature, but it's
very easy to lose sight of just how human he really was. This
verse definitely drives home the message. Because of his love
for us, Christ allowed himself to experience many of the inconveniences we face each day. He knows what it's like to be
tired, hungry, and sad. If we study his life and get to know
him personally, we'll have a great example to follow. He not
only knows what you face each day, he can show you how to
rise above the pain of being human and always do the will
of the Father.

*Thank you for becoming human, Jesus. Fill me with
your grace and teach me to follow in your footsteps.*

JUNE 29

"Do not call conspiracy all that this people call conspiracy, and do not fear what they fear, nor be in dread." (Isaiah 8:12)

The world provides many opportunities for anxiety. Sickness, death, financial instability, violence, and natural disasters are often causes of excessive worry. As Christians, however, we have an advantage. Our God is bigger than any of these potential calamities, and none of them can jeopardize the promise of eternal life.

So why do we let these things bother us so much? Chances are it's because we spend more time dwelling on earthly matters than on God's promises. While I'm not recommending that you bury your head in the sand and ignore what is going on in the world, I do recommend that you get in the habit of spending some time focusing on God each day. There are many nights when instead of watching television before bed, I read my Bible. I'm always amazed at how much peace I feel from just ten minutes of reading God's Word.

Almighty God, you are bigger than all of the world's problems. Instead of watching the daily news tonight, I'll spend some time reading your Good News.

JUNE 30

"Do not be afraid, Paul." (Acts 27:24)

One of the difficulties faced by Christians who suffer from anxiety is excessive guilt. This guilt often grows because of the comments of well-meaning individuals who attribute fear to a lack of faith. As illustrated by the words of the angel to St. Paul (who happens to be a saint), even the holiest of people were afraid at times!

When I give parish talks about anxiety, I always make the point that it's perfectly acceptable to be afraid. Fear is an emotion; it is not sinful. I have learned to let my fear lead me to Christ, and I recommend that you do the same. Your fear will decrease as you grow closer to him. In the meantime don't be afraid to be afraid!

Sometimes I feel afraid, Jesus. Teach me to view my fear as a reminder to turn to you in faith.

JULY 1

"Truly I say to you, whoever says to this mountain, 'Be taken up and cast into the sea' and does not doubt in his heart, but believes that what he says will come to pass, it will be done for him." (Mark 11:23)

For many years I was employed as a software developer. Over time the nature of the job caused me to become somewhat cynical and pessimistic. Even the best developers are well aware that very few programs work correctly the first time they are tested. As a result successful outcomes can be shocking.

Unfortunately many of us take the same approach with our prayers. We pray halfheartedly and are amazed when God comes through for us. In this verse Jesus is encouraging us to believe in his power to answer our prayers. The Bible is filled with stories of miracles that God worked in the lives of ordinary people who believed. Reading these accounts will help you to realize what he can do in your life.

Jesus, I believe you truly can do all things. Remove any doubt from my heart and fill me with confidence!

JULY 2

Why are you cast down, O my soul, and why are you disquieted within me? Hope in God; for I shall again praise him, my savior and my God. (Psalm 43:5)

What makes you sad? Bad weather? Boredom? Illness? Loneliness? There are many events in life that can rob us of happiness if we're not careful. On the other hand, we have the ability to find joy even when things aren't going our way. The secret is to stay focused on God.

No matter what happens in your life, there is always hope. Through Jesus Christ you have the opportunity to live forever in heaven. No earthly problem can take away that offer. Focusing more on God's promises and less on your problems is the key to experiencing happiness.

Dear Jesus, thinking about the joy of spending
eternity with you instantly lifts my spirits and
makes my problems seem less severe. Teach me to
focus more on you and less on my difficulties.

JULY 3

*But he withdrew to the wilderness
and prayed. (Luke 5:16)*

Jesus was busy . . . *very* busy! With miracles to be performed and lessons to be taught, he was always on the go. Well, not always. Despite the fact that he led a very active life, Jesus carved out time to converse with his Father in prayer. We should pay attention and follow his example.

As a self-employed speaker and author, I can easily fall into the trap of working nonstop. But that would be a disastrous move on my part. Without God's help not only would my work fall apart, but so would my life. Jesus understood the importance of prayer and took time out of his busy schedule to pray. No matter how much you have on your plate, you're not busier than Jesus. If he could find time to pray, so can you.

*Jesus, sometimes I rush around so much that I
forget how important it is to spend time with you.
I will make an effort to pray throughout the day.*

JULY 4

The Lord will rescue me from every evil and save me for his heavenly kingdom. To him be the glory for ever and ever. Amen. (2 Timothy 4:18)

Despite the fact that he faced numerous challenges, St. Paul never let anything stop him from proclaiming the gospel. In concluding his second letter to Timothy, Paul shares the secret of his persistence: He had complete trust in God's providence.

God has a plan for each of us. We all have a role to play in advancing his kingdom. By using our talents we can lead souls to Christ. Do you sometimes feel overwhelmed, thinking that you are weak or lack the strength to carry out your mission? Let Paul's words inspire you. If God asks you to do something, he will give you what you need to finish the job.

Jesus, sometimes I am too afraid of what others think to share the gospel with them. Grant me the grace necessary to persist, even when faced with opposition.

JULY 5

Jesus turned, and seeing her he said, "Take heart, daughter; your faith has made you well." And instantly the woman was made well. (Matthew 9:22)

As a rule of thumb, a large and complex project will take longer to complete than a smaller one. We generally accept this and attribute it to the fact that we are human and have limitations. Sometimes, however, we make the mistake of believing that God is bound by the same restrictions. The incident of the hemorrhaging woman illustrates that this is not the case.

After suffering for twelve years, the hemorrhaging woman was healed instantly by Jesus. All it took was for her to touch the fringe of his garment. Miraculous healings are not a big deal for Jesus. If he doesn't respond immediately or in the way that you desire, it doesn't mean he is weak or doesn't care. It means he knows what is best for you. Take comfort in this fact and always approach him with confidence.

I believe in your infinite power and wisdom,
Jesus. No matter how bleak things might
look, you are right here with me. I know
you can instantly answer my prayers.

JULY 6

At Gibeon the Lord appeared to Solomon
in a dream by night; and God said, "Ask
what I shall give you." (1 Kings 3:5)

One of the great spiritual mysteries is why God wants us
to ask for what we need. Doesn't he already know what we
need? Like it or not, however, that is the way he operates.
And because of apathy or lack of faith, we often fail to obtain
the many blessings God wants to give us.

The Lord's question to Solomon is one that we all need
to answer. What do you want God to do for you? What are
the pressing spiritual and material needs in your life? Ask
today for them to be fulfilled. You may be astonished to see
just how many blessings he plans to send your way.

Thank you for your willingness to satisfy
my desires, Lord. I will make it a point to
continually approach you with my requests.

JULY 7

Be strong and of good courage; be not frightened, neither be dismayed; for the Lord your God is with you wherever you go. (Joshua 1:9)

Make no mistake about it, Joshua had a tough job. God chose him to lead the Israelites into the Promised Land. And to ensure that fear would not stop him from carrying out this mission, he was given a much-needed pep talk. In this message God assured Joshua of his constant presence on the journey.

Just as it was for the Israelites, it's easy for us to lose sight of Christ's presence. The fact that we can't see him makes it challenging to remember that he is with us. Through faith, however, we are assured that this is indeed the case. Wherever you go and whatever you do, be strong and courageous.

God is with you!

No matter where I go and what I do, Jesus,
I am comforted by the thought that you are
with me. In you I am strong and courageous!

JULY 8

"Do not be afraid of them. Remember the Lord, who is great and terrible, and fight for your brethren, your sons, your daughters, your wives, and your homes." (Nehemiah 4:14)

For parents who tend to be anxious, raising children can be a great source of worry. As I travel around the country, I constantly meet parents who are worried about their children. Some are afraid of spiritual dangers and others worry about physical dangers, but the source of the anxiety is the same: the inability to protect their children from the threats around them. However, some things are out of our control, and trying to control the uncontrollable is guaranteed to produce anxiety. As frustrating as it can be to accept our limitations when it comes to protecting our children, there is someone who can help.

God loves your children even more than you do. He desires the best for them and is always willing to listen to your prayers on their behalf. Ask God the Father to protect your children from all spiritual and physical dangers. This is infinitely more effective than worrying about them.

Father, please protect my children from the dangers
they face. Always keep them close to you.

JULY 9

A man's mind plans his way, but the Lord directs his steps. (Proverbs 16:9)

It's been said that the best way to make God laugh is to tell him your plans. We all know the frustration that comes from unexpected challenges and failed ideas. As trying as this can be, however, it serves as a reminder that we are not in control. More important, it reinforces the idea that God always knows what is best.

Unless we learn to be flexible, we will never be peaceful. True happiness comes from submitting to God's will, even when it involves suffering or disappointment. He knows what we need to get to heaven and will often assist us in mysterious ways. While we don't have to understand everything that he does, we do need to trust him. That is how we find peace.

Grant me a greater desire to surrender to your will, God. I know this is the true path to the peace I seek.

JULY 10

Then Abraham fell on his face and laughed, and said to himself, "Shall a child be born to a man who is a hundred years old? Shall Sarah who is ninety years old, bear a child?" (Genesis 17:17)

When we think of Abraham, we generally don't picture him falling on his face and laughing. Considering the circumstances, however, it was a very understandable reaction. Even though this story turned out well, things weren't looking good for the patriarch and his wife. Abraham's reaction illustrates just how human he was.

Does the thought of laughing at God make you uncomfortable? Could it be too disrespectful? I don't see it that way at all. Abraham's great faith is well documented in the pages of the Bible. He never doubted that God would deliver on his promises. On the other hand, the fact that he was comfortable enough to laugh at God indicates that they had a close relationship. Do you feel that close to God? If not, it wouldn't hurt to laugh every now and then!

God, I desire to have a deeper relationship
with you. Remind me that it's okay to laugh
sometimes. Even as I face challenging situations,
give me a light heart, full of trust.

JULY 11

You ask and do not receive, because you ask
wrongly, to spend it on your passions. (James 4:3)

We don't always know why God denies our petitions, but St.
James offers one possible reason. Even if we have the best of
intentions, sometimes we ask God for things that will harm
us spiritually. Although it may not feel like it at the time, his
denial is actually a great blessing.

Behind all of our prayer requests should be a desire to
grow closer to Jesus. Because of our fallen human nature,
however, that does not always happen. We often confuse our
needs with our wants. There is no reason to fear, though.
While we should ask for the grace to desire only what God
wants us to have, we know that he won't give us anything
that could jeopardize our salvation. That is very good news.

God, you know what is best for me. Take
away from me the desire for anything except
what will draw me closer to you.

JULY 12

I know that you can do all things, and that no purpose of yours can be thwarted. (Job 42:2)

If we fully understood Job's words, we would spend much less time worrying. Lacking faith in God's power and mercy is a major source of anxiety, even among Christians. Often we don't realize that much of our worry is rooted in a lack of trust. Fortunately this is not a hopeless dilemma—our faith will increase if we focus on God's power.

Instead of dwelling on the problems we face, we should spend time reflecting on God's omnipotence. This simple verse from the Book of Job is a great place to start. Concentrating on God's power will help us to realize that there is no such thing as a hopeless situation. To God every problem is fixable. I feel better already. How about you?

Heavenly Father, your power is infinite. When I am discouraged or afraid, I will focus on the fact that no situation is beyond your control.

JULY 13

For the wages of sin is death, but the
free gift of God is eternal life in Christ
Jesus our Lord. (Romans 6:23)

We don't deserve to live forever in heaven. While that might sound harsh, it is a true statement. Because of the sins committed by mankind, death entered the world and the gates of heaven were closed. Due to God's mercy and the sacrifice of Jesus, however, we have been redeemed and heaven is once again a possibility.

Reflecting on God's free gift should make us feel very grateful. The realization that we can one day live forever in paradise makes our earthly problems seem a little less overwhelming. If you're struggling to make it through the day, take a few minutes to thank God for his generosity. He has given us a priceless gift.

Thank you, God, for your great generosity and
for sharing your heavenly kingdom with me.

JULY 14

His master said to him, "Well done, good and faithful servant; you have been faithful over a little, I will set you over much; enter into the joy of your master." (Matthew 25:23)

The parable of the talents (see Matthew 25:14–30) is one of Jesus' most familiar stories. At different points in my life, I have found it to be frightening, challenging, and uplifting. It really depends on how you look at it. In this captivating story, Jesus reminds us of the importance of using the talents that he gave us.

Let's focus on why this parable is so uplifting. Solely because of God's generosity, we are given the opportunity to enter into his joy. For those of us who tend to be anxious, this is a very comforting thought. As a result of Jesus' challenge, I want to make the most of my time here on earth, maximizing my talents and doing whatever it takes to ensure that I end up in heaven. It's a sweet deal. Don't pass it up!

Jesus, you have given me unique talents—
what I do matters. Even when I feel anxious
or afraid, let me share my gifts with others
instead of burying them in the ground.

JULY 15

Pour out your heart like water before the
presence of the Lord! Lift your hands to him for
the lives of your children. (Lamentations 2:19)

When my wife and I were faced with the possibility that
our twins would not be born alive, we truly put this verse
into practice. In addition to praying throughout the day, we
made it a point to pray a Rosary each evening. In addition
to praying for healing for Mary and Elizabeth, we prayed for
the grace to accept God's will.

As parents we sometimes feel helpless when it comes to
protecting our children. This verse reminds us that there is
always something we can do. Prayer is extremely effective
because it allows us to tap into the almighty power of our
heavenly Father. That is a million times more effective than
anything we can do on our own.

*Thank you for the gift of my children, Father. I
entrust them to your care. You love them more than
I ever could, and I know you will take care of them.*

JULY 16

Jesus said to him, "You have believed because you have seen me. Blessed are those who have not seen and yet believe." (John 20:29)

Throughout this book I have challenged you in many ways. My hope is that by being stretched a bit, you will grow closer to Jesus and experience his peace in a deeper way. In this particular meditation, I'd like to choose a somewhat different approach. I would like to congratulate you for believing in God's promises.

The fact that he is invisible makes it challenging to believe in God. Although we have the gift of faith to help us, we still have to exercise that gift. Reading this book implies that you are open to God showing you how to overcome your anxiety and experience his peace. Great job! Continue to present him with all your needs, even when they seem impossible to fulfill. That kind of faith will yield great results in your life.

I believe in you, God! I invite you
to work miracles in my life.

JULY 17

He was fifty-eight years old when he lost his sight, and after eight years he regained it. (Tobit 14:2)

I don't know about you, but I can be very impatient. Not only does my impatience show itself in my daily activities, but it also affects my prayer life. When I pray, I prefer God to answer immediately. The fact that he doesn't operate that way can be very frustrating. Can you relate?

In order to experience peace, either we have to change or God has to change. Since we all know that God doesn't change (that's why he's God!), you and I have to get busy. It all starts with accepting the fact that God always knows best. Tobit was healed after praying for eight years. What if he had stopped praying after seven? Let's continue to persevere and give God the benefit of the doubt when it comes to our prayer requests. His timing is perfect.

Jesus, teach me to persevere in prayer and
trust that your timing is always perfect.

JULY 18

> "If you then, who are evil, know how to give good gifts to your children, how much more will the Heavenly Father give the Holy Spirit to those who ask him!" (Luke 11:13)

When I was a teenager, minibikes were very popular. Despite the fact that these scaled-down motorcycles were not legal for street use, many of my friends had them. I repeatedly begged my parents for a minibike, but they refused. Their reasoning didn't make sense to me at the time. Illegal? Dangerous? I thought they were just being mean!

No matter how much we kick and scream, our heavenly Father will not give us something that will harm us. He loves us too much. Take comfort in that fact. And by the way, make it a point to thank him when your prayer requests are denied. Every time he says no, God is telling you that he loves you.

Father, thank you for saying no when I ask for things that could be dangerous. Even though I may not always understand, I trust that you know best. And thank you for the gift of the Holy Spirit!

JULY 19

As a deer longs for flowing streams, so longs
my soul for you, O God. (Psalm 42:1)

What are the longings of your heart? There is no need to panic if God isn't at the top of your list. Sometimes we become so confused by the temptations of the world that our desire for God gets buried.

We were all created with a desire for God's presence in our lives. You may not even realize that your desire for happiness is a manifestation of your yearning for God. Even if you don't believe it, try putting it into practice. Make the effort to encounter him through prayer, Scripture, and the sacraments each day and see what happens. You will discover that God is the only true source of happiness. If you have him, you have all you need.

Although I don't always realize it, God, I'm
really seeking you whenever I seek happiness.
Continue to reveal yourself to me each day.

JULY 20

And now, behold, I am going to Jerusalem,
bound in the Spirit, not knowing what
shall befall me there. (Acts 20:22)

For many people the future can be a frightening topic. Fear of the unknown can cause us to become anxious about events that may not even occur. I am very familiar with the what-if game; it has caused me much distress over the years. Every time we worry about the future, we are forgetting one important fact: The future may be unknown to us, but it's not unknown to God.

Because he believed in God's providence, St. Paul was willing to make the trip to Jerusalem even though potential danger awaited him. If you suffer from a fear of the future, I recommend that you look at the past. Reflecting on how many times Jesus has been there for you is a great way to face the future with confidence. If he was there for you yesterday, he will be there for you tomorrow.

Jesus, you know what the future holds for me.
Teach me to trust in your loving providence.

JULY 21

And the angel of the Lord appeared to the
woman and said to her, "Behold, you are
barren and have no children; but you shall
conceive and bear a son." (Judges 13:3)

The wife of Manoah (whose name is not recorded in the Bible) was barren. We don't know her feelings about this situation, but we do know that God sent an angel to deliver a message of hope. The angel's promise to Manoah's wife was indeed fulfilled, and she became the mother of Samson.

I don't like the word *hopeless*, and you shouldn't either. It implies that there is a limit to God's power, which is absolutely not true. God is all-powerful, and nothing is impossible for him. Don't ever stop believing in his power. He is bigger than any situation you will ever face. Always keep that in mind when you pray. No matter what anyone tells you, there is *always* hope!

God, no challenge is too big for you, and no situation
is hopeless. Open my eyes to your powerful presence
in my life and in the lives of those around me.

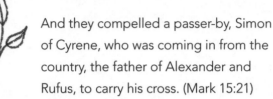

JULY 22

And they compelled a passer-by, Simon of Cyrene, who was coming in from the country, the father of Alexander and Rufus, to carry his cross. (Mark 15:21)

At first glance it appears that Simon of Cyrene was in the wrong place at the wrong time. He "just happened" to be passing by at the time Jesus needed help carrying his cross, and he was compelled by the authorities to lend a hand. With God, however, there are no accidents; this incident is actually an example of divine providence.

In his human state Jesus was too weak to carry the cross and needed help to complete his redemptive mission. Whether he knew it or not, Simon was God's instrument to lend a hand to Jesus. If you are struggling and need help, God has a Simon of Cyrene ready to come to your aid. Keep your eyes open and don't stop praying. Help is on the way.

God, thank you for the many "Simons" you have sent me through the years. Please continue to show me how to carry the crosses in my life. And teach me to recognize when you might be asking me to be a Simon in someone else's life.

JULY 23

Then he said to me, "Fear not, Daniel, for from the first day that you set your mind to understand and humbled yourself before your God, your words have been heard, and I have come because of your words." (Daniel 10:12)

When you've prayed for something and God hasn't seemed to be answering, have you ever reached a point where you've simply stopped asking? While this is a common response, it is not a good one. This verse reminds us that even if he doesn't respond immediately, God always hears our prayers and will answer when the time is right.

Although it can be frustrating, you can grow closer to God during periods of "unanswered" prayer. It gives you the opportunity to walk by faith and express your trust in his providence. Take comfort in the knowledge that God always hears your prayers. Most important, don't ever stop praying for what you need. When you are not getting a response, it's usually because he is up to something big!

Sometimes it feels like you are ignoring me, God.
Help me to be patient and trust in your timing.

JULY 24

You keep him in perfect peace, whose mind is stayed on you, because he trusts in you. (Isaiah 26:3)

It took me a long time, but I have learned an important lesson about overcoming anxiety. The more time I spend focusing on my problems, the more miserable I become. On the other hand, time spent thinking about Jesus always results in greater peace.

The Gospels are filled with stories of Jesus healing the sick, overcoming evil, and exhibiting unconditional love. Reading them will not only take your mind off of yourself, it will give you a glimpse of what Christ can do in your life. Furthermore, it will allow you to encounter him on a personal level. Take a break from worrying about your problems, open your Bible, read about Jesus, and see what happens. Making this a regular practice will put you on the road to peace.

Jesus, help me to appreciate the gift of sacred Scripture. Increase my desire to enter more deeply into your words and actions in the Gospels.

JULY 25

Therefore encourage one another and build one another up, just as you are doing. (1 Thessalonians 5:11)

Worrying excessively about our problems can cause us to become self-absorbed. As a result we may not be aware that there are people around us who are suffering. Even sadder is the fact that we could do something to ease the pain of those individuals.

St. Paul reminds us how important it is to encourage others and build them up. As worriers we are in the unique position of being able to empathize with others who are anxious, and we know how to help them. Often God will send such a soul into your life, giving you the opportunity to act on his or her behalf. Be on the lookout. You may get to bring God's peace into someone's life today.

Show me some ways I can encourage the people around me, God. Instead of being so wrapped up in my own worries, show me how I can brighten someone else's life today.

JULY 26

So Lot chose for himself all the Jordan valley,
and Lot journeyed east; thus [he and Abram]
separated from each other. (Genesis 13:11)

When Abram and his nephew Lot left their country and dwelt together, they began to experience conflict when it came to sharing the land. As a result Abram decided it would be better for them to part ways. He then allowed his nephew to choose where he wanted to settle. Seeing that the Jordan valley was well watered and fertile, Lot chose to move to Sodom. What seemed like a good choice ended up being disastrous, as Sodom eventually was destroyed because of its immorality.

By following God's instructions to the letter, Abram was fully protected. He knew God would provide and was even willing to let Lot have the first choice. If God wants something to happen, it will happen. We were created to live with him forever in heaven. All of the temptations and threats in the world can't change that. As long as we stay close to him and obey his commands, God will look out for us. That makes me very happy!

Thank you for the promise of eternal life, Father.
Teach me to always obey your commands.

JULY 27

To set the mind on the flesh is death,
but to set the mind on the Spirit is
life and peace. (Romans 8:6)

What does it mean to "set the mind on the flesh"? According to St. Paul those who do so are hostile to God and do not submit to his law (see Romans 8:7). All that matters to such individuals is the pursuit of pleasure. Living in this manner will not bring happiness here on earth or result in a heavenly reward.

On the other hand, following the Holy Spirit will provide joy in this life and eternal happiness in the next. While the choice seems obvious, very few of us set our minds solely on the flesh or solely on the Spirit. More often than not we bounce back and forth. Knowing that it will please God and bring you peace, get in the habit of praying for the grace to focus more on spiritual things. Doing so will increase your chances for success and bring you the peace you long for.

*Jesus, teach me to set my mind on
the things of the Spirit, not merely on
fleeting pleasures here on earth.*

JULY 28

"And you will hear of wars and rumors of wars; see that you are not alarmed; for this must take place, but the end is not yet." (Matthew 24:6)

If you're afraid that the crazy state of our world means the end is near, this verse should put your mind at ease . . . sort of. Jesus said we wouldn't be given advance notice of his second coming (see Matthew 24:36), and he warned us that he will return at an unexpected time (see Matthew 24:44). Therefore we need to be ready.

Instead of panicking about troubling events in the world and what they might signify, we should learn to live each day as if it is our last. By doing so we will be ready to meet Jesus either at the end of our lives or when he comes in glory, whichever comes first.

Thank you for encouraging me to be prepared,
Jesus. Rather than worrying about all the
troubling events taking place in our world, I
will focus on the big picture and concentrate on
living each day in readiness for your return.

JULY 29

And at the seventh time he said, "Behold, a little cloud like a man's hand is rising out of the sea." And he said, "Go up, say to Ahab, 'Prepare your chariot and go down, lest the rain stop you.'" (1 Kings 18:44)

Elijah believed in the power of prayer. That's why when praying for rain during a serious drought, he repeatedly sent his servant to look toward the sea for the rain that he knew was being sent. On the seventh attempt a little cloud could be seen rising out of the sea. Even though it was very small, Elijah knew that the much-needed rain was on the way.

Are you frustrated by unanswered prayers in your life? Be on the lookout for little ways God could be responding to your requests. You may not see the major rain you need, but you might observe the smallest of rain clouds, which indicates God is getting ready to send a downpour of blessings!

Father, instead of complaining about what you haven't done for me, I will focus on what you have done in my life. Thank you for showering blessings on me!

JULY 30

This, the first of his signs, Jesus did at Cana
in Galilee, and manifested his glory; and his
disciples believed in him. (John 2:11)

Jesus understands our tendency to believe what is seen more than what is unseen. Therefore he performed several miracles to help his followers believe in his power. Not only does his behavior illustrate a good understanding of human nature, it also shows his compassion. He makes every effort possible to help us believe in him.

If you are struggling to believe in God's power, get in the habit of reading about his miracles in the Gospels. Starting with turning water into wine at Cana and ending with his ascension into heaven, Jesus performed many miracles designed to strengthen our faith. In addition I recommend that you look back at the many times he has done miraculous things in your life. Spending time meditating on these events will increase your faith and give you greater hope for the future.

Thank you for the ways you turn water into wine
in my life, Jesus. I'm grateful for how you have
worked in my life, transforming me in the process.

JULY 31

Both riches and honor come from you, and
you rule over all. In your hand are power and
might; and in your hand it is to make great and
to give strength to all. (1 Chronicles 29:12)

Over the years I've had the opportunity to be present at the
taping of several television shows. In every case there was an
individual who was responsible for "warming up" the studio
audience. Prior to the taping, a series of jokes and interac-
tive routines would be used to ensure that the show would
receive a lively response from those in attendance.

King David knew a thing or two about preparing his
people for worship. By first acknowledging the greatness of
God, David ensured that the hearts of the people would be
in the right place when they prayed. It's critical that you and
I learn to do the same thing. Otherwise we could end up
forgetting just how much God can truly do in our lives. The
next time you pray, first spend some time dwelling on God's
power. I guarantee that you'll pray with greater confidence.

I praise you for your unlimited power, God.
When I think about how great you are,
my heart is filled with confidence!

AUGUST 1

After these things the word of the Lord came to Abram in a vision, "Fear not, Abram, I am your shield; your reward shall be very great." (Genesis 15:1)

After I purchased my smartphone, one of the first things I did was install a protective shield for the phone's screen. In case the phone is dropped (a very real possibility), the shield is designed to protect the delicate glass from shattering.

As fragile as smartphones can be, human beings are even more delicate. Furthermore, we are subject to many more dangers than just being dropped. Living in a world filled with temptation, we are definitely in need of protection. Just as he promised Abram that he would shield him from danger, God extends the same offer to each of us. You will face temptations every day, but do not be afraid. Ask God to shield you, and he will keep you safe.

God, just as you did with Abram, please
be my shield and protect me from
the dangers that surround me.

AUGUST 2

And he said, "Abba, Father, all things are possible to you; remove this chalice from me; yet not what I will, but what you will." (Mark 14:36)

If you are suffering and unsure of how to pray, these words spoken by Jesus are a good place to start. In one sentence he reminds us that:

- God can do all things.
- It's perfectly acceptable to ask God to take away our suffering.
- We should be willing to accept his answer, even if it's not what we want.

While there is nothing I can add to this message, I can vouch for the peace that will result if you pray in this manner.

I know that you can take away my suffering, Jesus.
I ask you to do so, but only if it is your will.

AUGUST 3

Do not neglect to do good and to share
what you have, for such sacrifices are
pleasing to God. (Hebrews 13:16)

Do you know how to please God? Sometimes it can be very
obvious, but not always. I have lived through many situations
when I was unsure of what God wanted me to do. This
dilemma can often be quite stressful.

In this verse we are reminded of the importance of doing
good and sharing what we have. By doing so we please God.
In all honesty I often find it much easier to open my prayer
book and sit in church than to do good deeds and share with
others—and I know I'm not alone. That's why this message
is included in the Bible. We have a tendency to want to serve
God in a way that feels good to us. Sometimes, however, he
wants us to serve him in a way that may be uncomfortable or
unpleasant. Let's pray for the grace to always seek to please
God.

God, sometimes I don't want to help others,
especially when it requires me to step out
of my comfort zone. Grant me the grace to
serve you in a way that pleases you.

AUGUST 4

Hannah also prayed and said, "My heart exults in the Lord; my strength is exalted in the Lord. My mouth derides my enemies, because I rejoice in your salvation." (1 Samuel 2:1)

To show gratitude to God for answering her prayers and granting her a child, Hannah offered these words of thanksgiving. In this heartfelt prayer, which many believe influenced Mary's Magnificat (see Luke 1:46–55), the grateful mother recognized God as the source of her strength. We would be wise to imitate her practice.

Too many times we become anxious and start to feel weak and overwhelmed. How will we get all our work done? How will we ever handle this problem? How can we possibly endure this suffering? The fact of the matter is that we *are* weak. In the game of life, however, weakness is not a deal breaker. God wants to help you with your struggles—every one of them. Let him be the source of your strength.

You are my strength, God. With you on my side,
I can deal with whatever comes my way each day.
Your presence in my life gives me confidence.

AUGUST 5

If you had walked in the way of God, you would be dwelling in peace for ever. (Baruch 3:13)

The best way to experience peace in life is to follow God's will. Because of our fallen human nature, however, this simple concept can be difficult to put into practice. But it is possible, and we should make it a priority.

What is God's will? He wants you to be holy and get to heaven. If you make this your main goal each day, you will be at peace. You will still have problems, and you may not always *feel* peaceful, but you will have peace of mind. In our pursuit of peace and happiness, we often overcomplicate matters. In the end walking with God is the ultimate answer.

God, I seek to do your will today. Grant me the grace
to remember this when my will gets in the way.

AUGUST 6

And Peter said to Jesus, "Master, it is well that we are here; let us make three booths, one for you and one for Moses and one for Elijah." (Mark 9:5)

Today the Church celebrates the Transfiguration, a feast that commemorates the glory of heaven. In order to build up their hope and help them deal with his upcoming crucifixion, Jesus gave Peter, James, and John a glimpse of what he would look like in his glorified state. Understandably Peter didn't want to leave and get back to reality, but it was necessary.

I frequently speak about the Transfiguration in my parish talks, because it teaches us an important lesson: We should get into the habit of thinking about the joy that awaits us in heaven. Otherwise we can easily become overwhelmed by the difficulties that we face every day. There is a light at the end of the tunnel, and it is a place of perfect happiness. Spend some time reflecting on that today.

Thank you for the gift of heaven, Jesus. I look forward to living there with you one day.

AUGUST 7

Many are the plans in the mind of a man, but it is the purpose of the Lord that will be established. (Proverbs 19:21)

No matter how unlikely or impossible it may seem at times, if God wants something to happen, it will happen. Even if you make bad decisions and your enemies sabotage your efforts, God can always bring good out of evil. Remembering this fact will save you from a great deal of unnecessary stress.

Because we have free will, we can always choose to do the wrong thing. Even when our actions are good, other people might thwart our efforts by doing evil. Instead of feeling defeated, however, we should rejoice in the fact that God is in charge. He can take any mess that we create and turn it into a masterpiece!

God, help me to remember that you can always bring good out of evil. I am grateful that even if I make a mess of things, you can create a masterpiece.

AUGUST 8

But the Lord answered her, "Martha, Martha, you are anxious and troubled about many things; one thing is needful. Mary has chosen the good portion, which shall not be taken away from her." (Luke 10:41–42)

The story of Martha and Mary has been confusing people for hundreds of years. What could possibly be wrong about being a gracious host for Jesus? Wasn't Mary being lazy by sitting at Jesus' feet while her sister worked herself into a frenzy? The answer can be found in Jesus' response to Martha's cry for help. While her actions were noble, she lost sight of *why* she was performing those actions.

In carrying out her duties, Martha became "anxious and troubled" because she was neglecting the spiritual nourishment Jesus could provide. Mary, on the other hand, understood the importance of spending time with Jesus. No matter how hectic your life is, make time to spend time with Jesus every day. Failure to do so will result in the same anxiety Martha experienced.

Sometimes I run around so much that I ignore you, Lord, caught up in my own worries and cares. I will make an honest effort to spend some time with you each day . . . even when I'm busy!

AUGUST 9

And by this we may be sure that we know him,
if we keep his commandments. (1 John 2:3)

How well do you know Jesus? In order to have a vital relationship with him, you have to know him first. And how can you be sure that you really know him? St. John provides us with a simple test to let us know if we're on the right track: We can be sure that we know Jesus if we keep his commands.

Rather than letting this discourage you, look at it as a call to action. This challenging verse gives us a plan for growing closer to Jesus. By avoiding sin and following his commandments, we have an opportunity to know him better. This should be a daily goal for each of us. If we continue to cooperate with his grace and fight to overcome our sinful inclinations, we will get to know him better each day.

Jesus, my desire is to know you better. I want to
do my best to avoid sin and grow closer to you.

AUGUST 10

For thus says the Lord God: Behold, I,
I myself will search for my sheep, and
will seek them out. (Ezekiel 34:11)

Several years ago my family and I attended a wedding in Cape May, New Jersey. During the cocktail hour one of my young daughters disappeared. My wife and I frantically searched for her, eventually finding her strolling down a deserted hallway. She was oblivious to the fact that Eileen and I were terrified and had been doing everything we could to locate her.

It's easy to feel like we're the ones searching for God. When many of us tell our conversion stories, we list the steps we took to find Jesus. While this is part of our journey, we can overlook an important fact: When we were lost and not overly concerned about finding God, that didn't mean he wasn't actively seeking us. Our heavenly Father loves us deeply and is always close by, even when we stray. Isn't it great to be loved so much?

*Thank you for always seeking me out, Jesus,
even when I'm oblivious to your presence. I
am grateful for your love and concern.*

AUGUST 11

Who shall separate us from the love of Christ? Shall tribulation, or distress, or persecution, or famine, or nakedness, or peril, or sword? (Romans 8:35)

We tend to view life's events as a series of blessings and curses, but this approach can get us into trouble. If we look at pleasant happenings as blessings from God and unpleasant occurrences as a sign of his displeasure, we are missing a critical point: *Everything* that happens to us is an expression of God's love.

St. Paul experienced an abundance of trials and tribulations, but he knew that nothing could ever separate him from the love of Christ. If you are facing adversity today, let this message comfort you. God loves you so much that he would never allow anything to happen in your life that would not benefit you in some way.

Jesus, it can be difficult to see your love in the unpleasant events of my life, but I know you love me— and you will never allow anything to separate us.

AUGUST 12

Instead you ought to say, "If the Lord wills, we shall live and we shall do this or that." (James 4:15)

Complaining about the weather is a popular activity. Depending on your personal preference, each new day can be too hot, too cold, too rainy, or too windy. And while I doubt it is intentional, every time we complain about the weather, we overlook the fact that God has blessed us with the gift of a new day. Because it has happened every day of our lives, we sometimes take for granted the fact that we will wake up in the morning.

Although it may seem like St. James is being a nitpicker, he makes a valid point. We often take God's blessings for granted, choosing instead to focus on our problems, our preferences, our comfort. Our self-centeredness can cause us to forget that we can do nothing without God willing it. Breathing, seeing, hearing, and waking up each morning are all his precious gifts to us. Let's not take them for granted.

God, I have so many plans, so many expectations.
Sometimes I forget that nothing happens unless you
will it. Thank you for the many blessings I often
take for granted. And thank you for the gift of today,
no matter what kind of weather we're having!

AUGUST 13

"When they deliver you up, do not be anxious about how you are to speak or what you are to say; for what you are to say will be given you in that hour." (Matthew 10:19)

Jesus knew that the apostles were not brave men, and he wanted to prepare them for the road ahead. Addressing the anxiety that could result from religious persecution, he assured them that they would receive supernatural help in their hour of need.

If Jesus assisted the apostles, he will also help us. Even though it may seem like we are fighting our battles alone, that is never the case. God will never allow us to face a single challenge without his assistance. It doesn't matter if it's religious persecution or financial difficulties. Jesus will always be there when we need him.

Thank you for your constant help with the challenges of life, Jesus. You are a true friend!

AUGUST 14

Lord, let me know my end, and what is
the measure of my days; let me know
how fleeting my life is! (Psalm 39:4)

A few years ago, I saw a roadside sign that read:

THE PROCRASTINATORS ANONYMOUS MEETING

HAS BEEN POSTPONED UNTIL NEXT MONTH.

Although the sign was intended to make people laugh, there
is a great deal of truth in that message. I tend to be a pro-
crastinator by nature, and as a result, I need deadlines. While
I don't enjoy the pressure of knowing that a project has to
be completed by a certain date, deadlines motivate me by
giving me a sense of urgency.

This prayer of the psalmist is a good one for two reasons.
First it reminds us that life is short. Second it helps us to appreciate the gift of the present moment. Many anxious individuals spend so much time worrying about tomorrow that
they miss today's blessings. The future is not guaranteed, so
why waste time worrying about it? Focusing on today will
bring you peace.

*God, our time here on earth is short. Teach me to live
one day at a time and not worry about the future.*

AUGUST 15

And a great sign appeared in heaven,
a woman clothed with the sun, with the
moon under her feet, and on her head a
crown of twelve stars. (Revelation 12:1)

Today we celebrate the Assumption of Mary into heaven. This is a great day to meditate on the fact that after her earthly suffering, Our Lady received her eternal reward. In addition it is comforting to realize that we have a heavenly Queen who can assist us with all our struggles in this world.

This verse helps me to picture the Blessed Mother sitting close to Jesus, waiting to lend a hand when I get in trouble. Just as my mother always kept a close eye on me when I was young, my heavenly Mother is constantly looking for ways to draw me closer to Jesus. Because she isn't pushy, however, Mary waits for us to approach her with our needs. Make it a point to do so today. Learning to seek her help was one of the best moves I ever made.

Holy Mary, Mother of God, pray for us sinners
now and at the hour of our death. Amen.

AUGUST 16

"Do not labor for food which perishes, but for the food which endures to eternal life, which the Son of man will give to you; for on him has God the Father set his seal." (John 6:27)

There is no doubt in my mind that if hundred-dollar bills were being given out at Mass, our churches would be packed. Even though we are given a gift far greater than money when we receive the Eucharist, there is something about material goods that is very attractive. God knows that we need money to survive in this life, but it should never be our main focus.

Pondering Jesus' words in this verse will help you to better appreciate the value of the Eucharist. Don't expect to appreciate its worth immediately, but give it time. Ask Jesus to help you understand the value of Holy Communion, and keep reading his words in the Gospels. You will gradually find your desire for this great gift increasing.

Jesus, thank you for the gift of the Eucharist. Please increase my desire to receive you as often as possible.

AUGUST 17

O Lord, you have searched me and
known me! (Psalm 139:1)

My wife knows me very well. In addition to knowing the
deep things (such as the way I think and believe), she knows
that I have a sweet tooth, and she will sometimes surprise
me by stopping at the bakery and purchasing my favorite
doughnuts. Every time she does this, Eileen is using her insight to express her love for me.

No matter how well Eileen knows me, God knows me
infinitely better. In fact, he knows me better than I know myself! Because of his perfect knowledge, God knows exactly
the kind of assistance I require to grow spiritually. When a
person challenges my patience or a trial arises that requires
me to trust, I know these things are all part of God's plan to
make me holy. Try thinking of this when difficulties arise in
your life. Every struggle that you face was handpicked just
for you.

You know me better than anyone ever could, Jesus.
Thank you for sending me the very things necessary
to transform me and build my character.

AUGUST 18

Woe to those . . . who trust in chariots because
they are many and in horsemen because they
are very strong, but do not look to the Holy
One of Israel or consult the Lord! (Isaiah 31:1)

As a new software developer, I struggled with many complex technical problems. Sometimes it took days or weeks, but eventually the solution would come to me. Over time I realized that I could solve these issues much quicker by swallowing my pride and asking more experienced colleagues for help.

As we struggle to solve life's problems, we often feel like it's all up to us. That sort of mentality not only illustrates a lack of humility, it's not based in reality. With God in our lives, we are never alone. Furthermore, he longs to provide us with all the resources necessary to deal with the issues we face each day. Whether you're struggling to balance the budget or to control a house full of noisy children, God wants to help you. Don't try to do it all by yourself.

*Thank you for caring about the details of my life,
God, and for always being available to me. When I
find myself worried and anxious, I will ask you for
help with the small things, as well as the big things.*

AUGUST 19

For you did not receive the spirit of slavery to fall back into fear, but you have received the spirit of sonship. (Romans 8:15)

One of the greatest sources of fear is the belief that we will never be able to conquer our sinful desires. If not addressed, this attitude can lead to despair. We can get to the point where we simply don't believe we can overcome our sinfulness.

In his letter to the Romans, St. Paul reminds us what a powerful ally the Holy Spirit can be in this area. With the help of the Spirit, we are no longer slaves to sin. Even though we have a fallen human nature, the Holy Spirit can enable us to rise above our sinful desires and live holy lives. There is no need to be afraid. With the assistance of the Holy Spirit and the grace received from the sacrament of confession, we can break free from the bondage of sin and lead a life pleasing to God!

Come, Holy Spirit. Fill me with your holy presence, and give me the power to overcome the sinful tendencies that weigh me down.

AUGUST 20

"Behold, I am the Lord, the God of all flesh; is anything too hard for me?" (Jeremiah 32:27)

Anytime we begin to worry, it is because we fail to trust in God. We are afraid that he isn't listening, isn't able to fix our problems, or isn't willing to give us the grace to deal with whatever we are facing. This Bible verse is one that should be highlighted and memorized, because it provides the answer to all of our fears.

Whenever I slip up and begin to worry, meditating on God's power and unconditional love always gets me back on track. He can give me the proper perspective regarding any situation in my life, and he loves me so much that he will respond to my prayers in the best way possible.

God, your power is without limit. Free me from unnecessary worry and increase my trust in your ability to handle the challenges I face.

AUGUST 21

I have fought the good fight, I have finished the
race, I have kept the faith. (2 Timothy 4:7)

There is definitely something to be said for milestones.
Whether it relates to my writing, family responsibilities, or
spiritual matters, I like being able to check off completed
tasks. As helpful as this technique can be, however, it is important that our milestones are realistic.

If your goal is to get through the rest of your life without worrying, you will quickly become overwhelmed and
defeated. If, on the other hand, you decide to trust God for
a few hours or for the duration of the crisis at hand, you'll
have a much better chance of achieving your goal and feeling satisfied. It's all about taking baby steps. Sometimes even
one day at a time can be too much for us. This is when we
should learn to trust for one hour (or one minute) at a time.

You know how often I struggle to trust you, Jesus.
Instead of promising to never worry for the rest of
my life, I will concentrate on not worrying today.

AUGUST 22

> "Watch and pray that you may not enter
> into temptation; the spirit indeed is willing,
> but the flesh is weak." (Mark 14:38)

Those of us who have a tendency to worry typically like to be in control. But wanting to control everything leads us to forget about the power of prayer. Because we can't always see the immediate results of our prayers, we often choose to run around and "do something" because it makes us feel better.

Jesus understands the value of prayer and reminds us that it is an effective weapon against all temptation, including the temptation to worry. As soon as you feel yourself beginning to worry, it's always a good idea to say a prayer. While it may seem unnatural at first, it will eventually become a reflex action. Even if you slip and start worrying again, your prayer will make a difference. Just before being taken into captivity, Jesus prayed in the Garden of Gethsemane. There are many other things that he could have done, but he chose to pray. It was not an accident.

Help me to appreciate the power of prayer, Jesus. I
have had a habit of worrying long enough; I choose
now to develop the habit of praying instead.

AUGUST 23

"I am he who comforts you; who are you that you . . . have forgotten the Lord, your Maker, and fear continually all the day because of the fury of the oppressor?" (Isaiah 51:12–13)

Watching the news these days can be pretty alarming. Seeing reports on terrorism, violent crime, and extreme weather eventually causes most of us to panic. However, secular news reports ignore one important fact: God is in charge. He is greater than any threat we could ever face.

This world is not a problem-free paradise. Natural disasters and evil actions are an everyday occurrence. Despite these threats, however, God is still in charge. He can calm the violent seas and turn situations around. Instead of being afraid, we should constantly turn to him and seek his intercession. We may never figure out why he allows certain events to happen, but we have the assurance that he is all-powerful. Instead of dwelling on the threats around you, place your hope in Christ, who can do all things.

God, I know that with you all things are possible.
Please keep me safe in this turbulent world.

AUGUST 24

I sought the Lord, and he answered me, and delivered me from all my fears. (Psalm 34:4)

What is the most common advice given to those of us who tend to worry? Just stop worrying! As easy as it is for a non-worrier to say, and as simple as it sounds, that recommendation is almost impossible to carry out. I should know—I have tried many times! On the other hand, it is entirely possible for a chronic worrier (like me) to experience peace. I speak from experience about this, too. The secret is to stop trying not to worry and start speaking to Jesus!

God answers all prayers without exception. If you ask him for something, you will get an answer. While I can't guarantee how or when he will answer, I know that he will. I also have learned that one of the first fruits of prayer is peace. Whenever I pray, I experience a sense of peace. Make it a point to seek Jesus daily; you will experience a peace that surpasses your expectations. Not only is it easier than trying to stop worrying—it's much more effective.

I am tired of living in fear, Jesus. I'm ready to experience the peace you promise. Thank you for always answering my prayers.

AUGUST 25

But Moses' hands grew weary; so Aaron and
Hur held up his hands, one on one side, and the
other on the other side; so his hands were steady
until the going down of the sun. (Exodus 17:12)

When the Israelites were attacked by the Amalekites, Moses
stood on the top of the hill and raised his hands in prayer.
As long as his hands were raised, Israel prevailed. When his
hands were down, Amalek had the edge. After Moses' hands
grew weary, Aaron and Hur supported his arms so they
would remain raised. Eventually Israel won the battle.

Intercessory prayer is very powerful. Asking others to
pray for us will get us through many difficult times. We also
can call on the saints and the souls in purgatory and ask for
their intercession. Don't make the mistake of trying to face
your problems alone. There are plenty of people on earth, in
heaven, and in purgatory who would love to help you!

Father, I am grateful for the gift of intercessory prayer.
Instead of facing my problems alone, I will make it a
point to turn to others for support and encouragement.

AUGUST 26

And the Lord said to Paul one night in a vision, "Do not be afraid, but speak and do not be silent." (Acts 18:9)

In the days of St. Paul, it was dangerous to be a Christian. While he was in Corinth, Paul faced many threats, and perhaps he was tempted to tone down his message in order to spare his life. Knowing the challenges the apostle faced, Jesus appeared to him and encouraged him to boldly continue sharing the Good News.

Even if we're not threatened physically, we sometimes avoid sharing our faith so we don't offend anyone or encounter resistance. We let the fear of ridicule or verbal harassment stop us from speaking up; as a result, we deprive others of the opportunity to hear the message of Christ. Let us heed the words of Jesus and always be willing to speak the truth when necessary. We could be saving someone's soul.

Jesus, you know how timid I can be when it comes to sharing my faith with others. Grant me the strength to speak the truth at all times, knowing that I may have just the words someone needs to hear.

AUGUST 27

On the evening of that day, the first day of the week,
the doors being shut where the disciples were, for
fear of the Jews, Jesus came and stood among them
and said to them, "Peace be with you." (John 20:19)

After rising from the dead, the first words of Jesus to his apostles were "Peace be with you." Considering that they were in hiding and afraid for their lives, it's highly likely that peace was something they lacked. How could they be peaceful during such a tumultuous time?

The beautiful thing about the peace of Christ is that it is supernatural. It can be experienced even in the midst of problems and suffering. By clinging to Jesus it is possible for us to be at peace even when our world seems to be falling apart. Turn to him each day in prayer and ask for his peace to fill your heart. No matter what you are facing, God can comfort you.

Thank you for a peace that is greater than any fear,
Jesus. Even in the midst of a challenging situation,
your peace can enfold me in a miraculous way.

AUGUST 28

The steadfast love of the Lord never ceases, his mercies never come to an end. (Lamentations 3:22)

As much as we try to love unconditionally, we fail far too often. We might be able to forgive someone once or twice, but eventually we reach our limit. God, however, doesn't operate that way; his love is unconditional. He is so merciful that he will never stop forgiving us for our sins.

This is a great meditation for you, especially if you're having a bad day. No matter what you are facing, you can take comfort in the fact that God loves you unconditionally. Nothing you can do will ever change that. If you think about it enough, you will start to feel very grateful. Eventually you may even forget about your worries and cares.

God, thank you for loving me unconditionally.
Teach me to extend mercy to others, showing
them a love without any strings attached.

AUGUST 29

But when he saw the wind, he was afraid,
and beginning to sink he cried out,
"Lord, save me." (Matthew 14:30)

Peter knew that it was not possible to walk on water. Still, he responded to the call of Jesus and discovered what happens when you place your trust in the one for whom all things are possible. As long as Peter kept his eyes on Jesus, he was indeed able to do the impossible and walk on water. When he focused on the wind, however, he became afraid and began to sink.

Every day we face challenges and obstacles that can rob us of the peace Jesus wants us to have. Focusing on your problems is a guaranteed way to become overwhelmed and stressed. On the other hand, if you make some time for Jesus each day, you'll have an altogether different focus—one that keeps things in perspective. Even a few minutes of prayer or reading your Bible at various intervals throughout the day will make a substantial difference. And when you slip up and become overwhelmed by your problems, imitate Peter and cry out, "Lord, save me!"

Jesus, I choose to keep my eyes on you, fully aware that you can help me to cope with whatever comes my way. With you, I can "walk on water"!

AUGUST 30

Abraham said, "God will provide himself the lamb
for the burnt offering, my son." (Genesis 22:8)

Can you imagine how peaceful you would be if you had the
faith of Abraham? Even though he was asked to sacrifice his
son, he somehow knew it would work out for the best. In
this case God did indeed provide an animal for the sacrifice,
but it wasn't until after Abraham was in the process of sac-
rificing Isaac.

Trusting in God's providence does not come easy for
many of us. To make matters worse, God often asks us to
take the first step before he delivers on his promise. That
is precisely how we grow in faith. Fortunately you can read
through the entire Bible and not discover one instance when
God failed to deliver on a promise. Everything he ever promised has either happened or is in the process of happening.
Placing your trust in him is always a good move.

Thank you for your faithfulness, Father.
Teach me to trust in your providence,
knowing that you will never fail me.

AUGUST 31

I can do all things in him who
strengthens me. (Philippians 4:13)

Do you believe you can do all things with Christ's strength?
Don't feel bad if you struggle with this question—most people do. It's one thing to believe it in theory, but it's another
thing to believe it when you find yourself dealing with financial distress, serious illness, or some other mountain in your
life. Paul certainly faced his share of ordeals and seemingly
insurmountable situations.

If God puts you into a difficult situation, he will give you
the grace to get through it. He will never allow you to experience more than you can bear. Of course, this doesn't mean that
you will never suffer. However, God will bring good from any
suffering that does come your way. You and I may never fully
understand why God does what he does. But we can understand that he loves us, strengthens us, and never gives us more
than we can handle.

*Jesus, thank you for giving me the grace to deal with any
problem that comes my way. It gives me such confidence
to say with Paul, "I can do all things" in you!*

SEPTEMBER 1

There is a way which seems right to a man, but its end is the way to death. (Proverbs 16:25)

Just because I think I'm doing the right thing doesn't mean that I am. The Church teaches that even if I follow my conscience, it is possible for me to commit an evil act. Why? Because my conscience could be wrong. That's why it is critical that my conscience is informed.

Two thousand years ago Jesus Christ founded his Church. Through Christ and his Church, we receive the grace necessary to get to heaven. The Church also provides us with the moral instruction we need to make good choices in life. We can't get to know Jesus while ignoring the teachings of the Catholic Church. He still speaks through his Church—and that's a good thing!

I will continue to seek your guidance through the Church, Jesus. Thank you for the many resources the Church provides to strengthen my faith and help me to grow spiritually.

SEPTEMBER 2

And when the sabbath was past, Mary Magdalene, and Mary the mother of James, and Salome, bought spices, so that they might go and anoint him. (Mark 16:1)

Did you ever become discouraged, thinking that God had abandoned you, only to discover that he really did answer your prayer? That is what happened to Mary Magdalene and her friend Mary as they went to the tomb of Jesus. They weren't there to see proof of his resurrection. Instead they came to anoint his dead body.

Just because God doesn't answer your prayers immediately doesn't mean that he won't come through. The fact that your life is a mess doesn't signify that God isn't hard at work. In fact, I have learned that turmoil in my life is often a sign that he is doing something powerful. Don't lose hope when things aren't going your way. God knows what he's doing, and he will never abandon you. Continue to pray and trust that he will act when the time is right.

God, sometimes I struggle to believe in your providence, and I feel discouraged and worried about the way things are going. Please grant me the grace to always believe that you know what is best for me.

SEPTEMBER 3

> For I, the Lord your God, hold your
> right hand; it is I who say to you, "Fear
> not, I will help you." (Isaiah 41:13)

For a frightened child, holding the hand of a parent brings great comfort. And as a parent I loved it when my daughters wanted to hold my hand. It brought me much joy to provide the security that they sought.

God doesn't want us to go through life alone. Nothing pleases him more than when we become like little children and reach for his hand. In addition to helping us with our problems, he wants to take our fear away. Don't let anyone tell you that it's impossible to go through life without ever being afraid. Reach for your heavenly Father's hand today. Just as he promised, he will indeed help you.

Heavenly Father, thank you for protecting me and
freeing me from my fears. I look forward to holding
your hand as we walk through life together.

SEPTEMBER 4

For he looked forward to the city which has foundations, whose builder and maker is God. (Hebrews 11:10)

Abraham's faith was so strong that he did whatever God asked of him. Even though he didn't know the final destination, he left his homeland and followed God. He was able to do so because he trusted that God would not mislead him.

We live in a world filled with distractions. It's very easy to lose sight of the fact that we were created for heaven. In order to keep our focus on spiritual realities, we must look beyond the instant gratification offered by material things. And material things (or lacking them) just as often lead to anxiety and worry. Instead, like Abraham, we can keep our eyes on God, trusting in his promises and following where he leads. It worked for Abraham, and it will work for you.

God, help me to remember that I was created for heaven. Although the world offers many attractions and distractions, only spiritual realities offer me lasting happiness, freedom from worry, and amazing peace.

SEPTEMBER 5

Samuel lay until morning; then he opened the
doors of the house of the Lord. And Samuel was
afraid to tell the vision to Eli. (1 Samuel 3:15)

Don't be afraid to be afraid. Because it is an emotion, fear is
morally neutral. It only becomes a problem if it prevents us
from doing what God wants us to do. Samuel received some
unpleasant news from God concerning Eli and his family.
And while he was afraid to present the bad news to Eli, he
overcame his anxiety and shared the message he had heard.

I have let fear stop me from doing the right thing many
times in my life. I'm not proud of that fact, but I can't change
the past. With the help of God's grace, instead of viewing
fear as a curse, I'm learning to see it as an opportunity.

Whenever you are afraid, recognize that you are being
given the chance to trust in Jesus. As you continue to take
advantage of these opportunities, you will find your fear de-
creasing and your faith increasing.

*God, grant me the strength to always do the right thing,
even when I am afraid. Thank you for the opportunity
to face my fears head-on and grow in faith.*

SEPTEMBER 6

My mouth is filled with your praise, and
with your glory all the day. (Psalm 71:8)

I have discovered that one of the best ways to start off my
day is by praising God. This is especially important when
I am struggling. When I am dealing with many problems,
I have a tendency to feel sorry for myself and focus on my
difficulties. Nothing cures me like praising God.

I recommend that you imitate the psalmist and get in
the habit of praising God throughout the day. Developing
the praise habit is a great way to move from dejection to joy.
Praising God and thanking him helps you to appreciate his
power and his presence in the midst of your problems.

God, I praise you for your power and
greatness, which far surpass any worries or
cares I might be dealing with today.

SEPTEMBER 7

And when the soles of the feet of the priests . . . shall rest in the waters of the Jordan, the waters of the Jordan shall be stopped from flowing. (Joshua 3:13)

When I was young I enjoyed ice skating. And while I typically would skate at a rink, I was able to do something unique one freezing winter day. The temperature was so low that a nearby creek was frozen solid, and my friends announced that they were going to skate on it. Even though I saw others skating on the ice, I still had doubts that it would support me. It wasn't until I stepped onto the ice that I felt confident that I wouldn't break through and fall into the frigid water.

Just as you will never learn to swim without jumping into the pool or learn to drive without getting in the car, you will never learn to trust God without stepping out in faith. In order to see what he can do in your life, you will generally need to take the first step. Is there an area where you feel that he is calling you to take the first step? Are you willing to set aside your doubt and uncertainty and do so?

God, I want to grow in faith, and I'm willing to take the first step. Help me to let go of my doubts and fears and trust that you will be there for me.

SEPTEMBER 8

But how are men to call upon him in whom they have not believed? And how are they to believe in him of whom they have never heard? And how are they to hear without a preacher? (Romans 10:14)

The world is filled with people who don't realize that it is possible to have a personal relationship with Jesus Christ. Furthermore, there are millions of individuals who are completely unaware that encountering Christ is the only way to experience lasting peace. What will it take for them to finally get it? It will take you and me telling them!

Worriers have a tendency to dwell on their own problems. Jesus, on the other hand, wants us to focus on the problems of others. By sharing Bible verses, words of encouragement, or even this book, you will help your friends, family members, and coworkers experience the peace God is longing for them to have.

Jesus, instead of being wrapped up in my own concerns, today I will make an effort to share your message with someone who is hurting or afraid.

SEPTEMBER 9

"I have said this to you, that in me you may have peace. In the world you have tribulation; but be of good cheer, I have overcome the world." (John 16:33)

Let's face it, having a close relationship with Jesus doesn't mean that you will not have problems. As much as we might like that to be the case, it simply is not. All you have to do is open the Bible and see that even those closest to Jesus suffered tremendously. On the other hand, remaining close to Jesus means that you will be able to experience peace. Even when you have problems? *Especially* when you have problems!

The peace Jesus gives is a supernatural peace, one that doesn't depend on external circumstances. It's a peace that exists even in the midst of problems. While that seems impossible to us, it is not impossible for God. He created the world and is bigger than any problem we could ever face.

Thank you for the gift of peace, Jesus. I will turn to you today and trust that you will give me rest.

SEPTEMBER 10

Fear not, O land; be glad and rejoice, for the
Lord has done great things! (Joel 2:21)

When I graduated from college, like many recent grads I struggled to get a job. My greatest obstacle was my lack of experience. Eventually an employer took a chance on me, and I began to gain valuable work experience. As a result each of my future job quests got a bit easier.

God has plenty of experience doing the impossible. A look through the pages of the Bible illustrates just how amazing he can be. Therefore you and I can learn to trust him to fix any situation we encounter. No matter what you are facing, God has dealt with a similar problem in the past and has come through with flying colors. Spend some time reflecting on his accomplishments today. Just like the prophet Joel, you'll end up rejoicing.

You have done amazing things throughout
history, God, and I am confident you can
do amazing things in my life, too.

SEPTEMBER 11

But the angel said to him, "Do not be afraid,
Zechariah, for your prayer is heard, and your
wife Elizabeth will bear you a son, and you
shall call his name John." (Luke 1:13)

Human beings can be very stubborn at times. After being told that God had answered his prayers, Zechariah refused to believe the good news. And while many of us will find fault with his lack of trust, how often do we react in a similar way? Instead of saying, "Thank you, Lord," we either question his actions or complain about how he answers our prayers.

God does a really good job of being God. Throughout the years he has proven himself time and time again. As much as we'd like to help him out, our efforts would be better spent learning to follow his will and thanking him for his unending mercy. For instance, you might start by expressing gratitude for waking up this morning, and then make an effort to appreciate all he does for you throughout the day. If you're at a loss for words, "Thank you" is a good place to start.

Thank you for answering my many prayers
through the years, God. Teach me to be
more aware of your kindness to me each
day and to learn to appreciate it fully.

SEPTEMBER 12

I will instruct you and teach you the way
you should go; I will counsel you with
my eye upon you. (Psalm 32:8)

When I was a child I didn't enjoy writing thank-you notes for birthday gifts. I struggled to come up with the words to express my gratitude. In an effort to help me, my mother would write a sample that I could follow. This made the process much easier for me.

Do you ever struggle with your prayers, wishing you could better express your feelings to God? While it's always acceptable to say anything that comes to mind, some of us could use a little extra help. One of the most helpful prayer tools I've discovered is the Book of Psalms. There is a psalm for every imaginable emotion. Best of all, these prayers are inspired by the Holy Spirit. If you're not sure where to start, try praying the responsorial psalm from daily Mass. (The daily Mass readings can be found online at usccb.org.) As you become more familiar with the psalms, you'll be able to choose the one that best suits your needs on any given day. You might be inspired to write your own psalm to God!

I am grateful for the gift of the psalms, God. Praying them
helps me to express the deepest feelings of my heart to you!

SEPTEMBER 13

Let us then with confidence draw near to the throne of grace, that we may receive mercy and find grace to help in time of need. (Hebrews 4:16)

Be totally honest: How much confidence do you have in God's ability (and willingness) to provide for your needs? Those of us who tend to be worriers usually have some trust issues. But just as we often must feel pain before we realize we should see a doctor, recognizing a lack of faith is an important first step in the conversion process.

Based on what I have seen in my life, I should have greater confidence in Christ. Why then do I struggle with trust at times? I believe that it primarily stems from a lack of awareness. I might concentrate so much on my problems that I forget about God's mercy and omnipotence. This verse from the Book of Hebrews, however, points me in the right direction. We can confidently come to God expecting to receive mercy and grace whenever we need it.

I know you can do all things, God, but sometimes my heart doesn't believe it. I will continue to relinquish my worry and give you the opportunity to provide for all my needs. Thank you for your mercy and grace!

SEPTEMBER 14

Then David said to Solomon his son, "Be strong and of good courage. . . . Fear not, be not dismayed; for the Lord God, even my God, is with you. He will not fail you or forsake you." (1 Chronicles 28:20)

I have a confession to make. Every time I sign a contract to write another book, my initial reaction is one of panic. Fortunately the duration and severity of my anxiety has decreased with each of the books I have written, but it is still there. Why? In all honesty the main reason I panic is that I worry about meeting the deadline.

While there is no doubt that writing requires self-discipline and talent, it also requires a great deal of inspiration from the Holy Spirit. I am still a work in progress, and I am learning just how powerful God's assistance can be. Are you struggling with your job? Are you overwhelmed with family responsibilities? Turn to God and ask for assistance. Whether it's writing a book, meeting a sales quota, or raising children, God will not bring you to a situation without helping you to get through it.

God, I know you will always give me the grace I need to deal with any situation I encounter in life. Instead of worrying, I will be strong and courageous in you.

SEPTEMBER 15

For this slight momentary affliction is preparing
for us an eternal weight of glory beyond
all comparison. (2 Corinthians 4:17)

When I was in my twenties, I used to lift weights regularly. I really didn't enjoy going to the gym, but I did feel good about being in shape. Although I wasn't a particularly disciplined person, I was able to look beyond the momentary discomfort and see the long-term benefits of exercise.

Many of our duties and situations in life can be categorized as mundane or even painful, but they can produce much fruit. Each time we offer up our suffering or dedicate our work to God, we make a deposit into the Bank of Heaven. The interest we will earn is better than anything we could ever get on earth!

*God, teach me to remember that all of my suffering
and inconveniences can be used to bear great
fruit for your kingdom, here and in eternity.*

SEPTEMBER 16

And he said to them, "Take nothing for your journey, no staff, nor bag, nor bread, nor money; and do not have two tunics." (Luke 9:3)

It's amazing how easy it is to trust God when you have money in the bank. Thinking back on my days as a software developer with a comfortable income, I don't remember ever worrying about money. I knew that I would be able to pay my mortgage and handle unexpected bills. My trust wasn't really in God—it was in my bank account!

God doesn't want us to be irresponsible, but he does want us to trust in his providence. That can be difficult if we have too many possessions. We need to find the proper balance, which is possible if we speak with him frequently. How much you should keep in savings and how much you should share with others are questions you should bring to Jesus. I can't give you a magic formula, but I do know this: Seeking comfort in money and possessions instead of in God is a big mistake.

God, I want to trust in your providence.
Please show me if I am placing too much
trust in the things of the world.

SEPTEMBER 17

Then the Lord appeared to Abram, and said,
"To your descendants I will give this land."
So he built there an altar to the Lord, who
had appeared to him. (Genesis 12:7)

At first glance God's message to Abram doesn't seem like a big deal. Abram was a good man, so the promise of land to his descendants appears to be a reasonable gesture. What makes this promise astonishing is that Abram was seventy-five years old and childless when God spoke these words to him.

All too often we place limits on God's power. We view situations as hopeless and problems as uncorrectable, completely ignoring God's involvement. Don't make the mistake of thinking that he can't answer your prayers. He can. Turn to him today and give him a chance.

No situation is hopeless to you, God; no obstacle
too big for you to tackle. I place all my problems
in your hands—and leave them there.

SEPTEMBER 18

Every word of God proves true; he is a shield to those who take refuge in him. (Proverbs 30:5)

These words are music to my ears. The thought that every word of God proves true is very comforting to me. After being subject to many broken promises and lies over the years, it's refreshing to know that someone always speaks the truth and keeps his word. That "someone" is God.

When I read though God's words in Scripture, I get excited when he promises that he will give me rest, answer my prayers, and save a place for me in heaven. My heart begins to race as he assures me that he forgives my offenses and will stay with me always. What makes all of these promises so special is that they are all true!

Thank you for always speaking the truth, God. I know I can believe every word you say. I take refuge in you!

SEPTEMBER 19

"For he who is mighty has done great things
for me, and holy is his name." (Luke 1:49)

Mary understood that she would play a critical role in salvation history. As this verse implies, she was very aware of God's grace working in her life. She knew that none of her accomplishments would have been possible without his supernatural help.

As Mary did, make it a point to thank God for the great things he has done for you. I have learned from experience that getting into this habit can quickly turn a "why me" mentality into an "attitude of gratitude." The mere fact that God created us is something to be thankful for. Acknowledging all the blessings he showers on us each day helps us to feel some of the gratitude Mary experienced as she expressed her appreciation. No doubt about it, God has done great things for each of us. Let us give thanks!

Mary, help me to appreciate all that God has done for me. I long to be filled with the same sense of humble gratitude you showed when you were on earth.

SEPTEMBER 20

Your word is a lamp to my feet and a light to my path. (Psalm 119:105)

Not knowing what God wants you to do can be stressful. You might agonize over making a decision that pleases God. You might think, *What if I make the wrong choice? What if I'm doing what I want instead of what God wants? What if I can't handle what he is asking me to do?* Questions like these can lead to paralysis and worry.

Fortunately for us, there is something we can do so making decisions is easier. As Catholics we believe that God speaks through sacred Scripture and sacred tradition. In the pages of the Bible and the teachings of the Church we hear God's voice and can let him guide us through the decision-making process. God has never been known for deserting his people, and he isn't going to start with you. Open your Bible, grab your *Catechism*, and pray for assistance to choose the option that pleases him. Be patient and the answer will come.

I want all my actions to please you, God. Teach me to always make decisions according to your will.

SEPTEMBER 21

"My Spirit abides among you;
fear not." (Haggai 2:5)

Maybe it's because I have a poor sense of direction, but I believe GPS is one of the greatest inventions of all time. It has taken away much of the fear that used to accompany me when I had to drive to an unfamiliar location. With my GPS by my side, I know that I will eventually arrive at my destination. If I do happen to make a wrong turn and get lost along the way, I know it is only a temporary setback.

Through the sacraments of baptism and confirmation, we receive the Holy Spirit and all his gifts. Similar to the help provided by a GPS, the Spirit offers assistance for living a holy life. As a result, we don't have to be afraid that our weaknesses will prevent us from acting in a manner that pleases God. Just as your GPS helps you to arrive at your final destination, so does the Holy Spirit. He will guide you on your spiritual journey as long as you listen to his promptings.

Holy Spirit, continue to guide me as I navigate
the often confusing and sometimes treacherous
road of life. Thank you for your constant help.

SEPTEMBER 22

They said to him, "We only have five loaves here and two fish." (Matthew 14:17)

How many times have you faced a situation and panicked because you didn't think you could handle what was being asked of you? I have been in that predicament many times over the course of my life, but I recently learned an important lesson. Doing something, even though it may not be much, eases my anxiety and makes the challenge seem a little less intimidating. It also gives Jesus the chance to multiply my meager efforts and find a positive solution.

Jesus could have created the food to feed the five thousand out of thin air, but he chose not to. Instead he asked his followers to give him what little food they had, and then he miraculously multiplied it. You may not feel you have what it takes to get past the mountain in front of you, but don't let it stop you from doing something. Even if you can't do something physical, you can always pray. Although it may not feel like it at the time, prayer is the most powerful action you could ever take.

Jesus, I will not panic when facing a crisis. Instead I will do whatever I can and trust that you will take care of the rest.

SEPTEMBER 23

You came near when I called on you; you
said, "Do not fear!" (Lamentations 3:57)

A few years ago I was looking over my notes for a talk I was
giving that evening, when I was overcome by a crushing pain
in my side. Hoping it would pass, I tried to keep working.
Eventually I gave up and asked my wife to drive me to the
emergency room. The pain was so severe that I begged the
ER doctor to do something to reduce it. He assured me that
not only would he be able to reduce my pain, but he would
take it away entirely. He was right.

That was the day I learned just how painful a kidney stone
can be. I also experienced the comfort of meeting someone
who could make that pain disappear.

Why should we listen to God's words when he tells us
to have no fear? Because he is powerful enough to take away
our anxiety. Turn to him and ask for help. He will not desert
you.

*You tell me not to fear, not to worry, God, and
these words bring me comfort and courage.
Whenever I am afraid, I will cry out to you,
knowing you will answer me swiftly.*

SEPTEMBER 24

O the depth of the riches and wisdom and knowledge of God! How unsearchable are his judgments and how inscrutable his ways! (Romans 11:33)

Unless I make a conscious decision to reflect on the power of Christ each day, I am extremely likely to panic whenever I face a crisis, for one simple reason: If I lose sight of God's power, even briefly, I will fail to recognize that he can come to my aid in times of danger.

St. Paul understood the power of God, and as a result, he was able to face many threatening situations with confidence. There is no doubt that many of God's actions are difficult to understand. Why was the Crucifixion necessary? Why did Jesus choose such weak individuals to be his apostles? Why did it take thousands of years for the Messiah to arrive? All these questions remind us that God's ways are not our ways. We won't always be able to understand his actions. That's okay. He really does know best.

You are all-powerful and all-knowing, God. I will continue to trust you even when I don't understand your actions.

SEPTEMBER 25

"Do not fear what you are about to suffer. Behold, the devil is about to throw some of you into prison, that you may be tested. . . . Be faithful unto death, and I will give you the crown of life." (Revelation 2:10)

I don't enjoy suffering. As a matter of fact, I am afraid to suffer. Despite my fear, however, I recognize that much good has resulted from the suffering I have endured over the years. In addition I know that God has always helped me to get through all the unpleasant experiences that I have faced.

Like it or not, suffering is a part of life. While we may not always be able to understand the reason for it, we know that there *is* a reason. We also know that God will never abandon us or give us more than we can handle.

Jesus, I trust in you.

SEPTEMBER 26

Behold, I send an angel before you, to guard you on the way and to bring you to the place which I have prepared. (Exodus 23:20)

Let's be honest—God knows us really well. Not only does he know our strengths, he also understands our weaknesses—all of them. In the Old Testament we read time and time again about how God dealt with the weaknesses of his chosen people. In order to help the Israelites keep their focus and reach the Promised Land, God sent an angel to accompany them and lead the way. If he assisted them, why wouldn't he do the same for us?

You may be facing many challenges today. As a result you could easily become distracted and lose sight of your main job—to follow God's will. Fortunately he has given you the sacraments, the Bible, a guardian angel, the saints, and other people to help you stay on the right path. Don't make the mistake of walking through life alone. Let God assist you!

God, thank you for all the assistance you provide
for me each day. Teach me to become more aware
of the spiritual resources available to me.

SEPTEMBER 27

Jesus said to them, "I am the bread of life; he who comes to me shall not hunger, and he who believes in me shall never thirst." (John 6:35)

Without physical nourishment our bodies would not be able to survive. In addition to its health benefits, food can be a source of enjoyment. But no matter how delicious a meal may be, it cannot bring us lasting happiness.

In chapter 6 of John's Gospel, Jesus reveals that he is the bread of life. When we consume his Body and Blood, all of our spiritual needs are fulfilled. Intimacy with Christ is the only way we can experience lasting peace. When I am stressed or worried, nothing makes me feel better than receiving Jesus in Holy Communion or spending time in his real presence. Make the time to be with Jesus today. He will nourish your spirit and fill you with his peace.

Thank you for feeding me with food that truly satisfies, Jesus. May I always appreciate your generosity and the gift of your presence in the Eucharist.

SEPTEMBER 28

Wait for the Lord; be strong, and let your heart take courage; yes, wait for the Lord! (Psalm 27:14)

Patience does not come naturally to most of us. I don't like to wait, but I understand that it can be beneficial. As someone who is prone to impulse buying, I have learned to delay making unnecessary purchases. By doing so I often lose interest in the item and end up saving money.

Learning to wait on the Lord not only develops patience, it also brings us peace. How often do you become angry and unsettled when God doesn't answer your prayers fast enough? Instead of losing your peace over God's delayed response, look at it as an opportunity to trust him. Focus on the fact that he loves you, that he knows best, and that he is all-powerful. If your prayers have not yet been answered, keep praying and trust that he is up to something big!

Father, you love me and only desire the best for me. Help me to learn patience and calmly wait for your timing, instead of rushing ahead of you or demanding immediate gratification.

SEPTEMBER 29

Keep your life free from love of money, and be content with what you have; for he has said, "I will never fail you nor forsake you." (Hebrews 13:5)

Show me someone who is content with what he or she has and I'll show you a peaceful person. While envy of the lifestyles of the rich and famous is an obsession in today's world, it is also a recipe for misery. If you want to make yourself miserable, the best way to do it is to focus on what you don't have. On the other hand, learning to be content with what you do have is certain to increase your peace.

Sometimes it's difficult to distinguish our *needs* from our *greeds*, but God never promised to satisfy our every whim. Instead he promised to give us what we need. Want to be peaceful? Pray for the grace to be content with what you have.

Jesus, sometimes I can't tell my needs
from my greeds. Grant me the grace to
always be content with what I have.

SEPTEMBER 30

"Only fear the Lord, and serve him faithfully with all your heart; for consider what great things he has done for you." (1 Samuel 12:24)

In his farewell address Samuel reminded the Israelites that one kind of fear is actually a good thing. In its purest sense, fear of the Lord is rooted in love. That is why the prophet recommended that the people consider what God had done for them. The more we think about God's goodness, the more we will love him and want to obey his commands.

Starting with the fact that he redeemed us, we could easily come up with a long list of the great things God has done for us. Why not make this a part of your daily spiritual routine? Every morning make a list of five things God has done for you. Try not to repeat yourself, and see how large your list becomes. Doing this on a regular basis will increase your desire to please him who loves you so much.

Considering all that you have done for me makes me very grateful, God. Teach me to please you at all times.

OCTOBER 1

And many rebuked him, telling him to be
silent; but he cried out all the more, "Son of
David, have mercy on me!" (Mark 10:48)

We all encounter people from time to time who tell us we're
being unrealistic when we place our faith in God. Occasionally we may even be the ones who dash someone's hopes.
Bartimaeus, a blind man, knew that Jesus could heal him,
and he wasn't about to let anybody stand in his way.

Jesus Christ performed many miracles that are documented in the pages of the Bible. He wants to perform mir
acles in your life today. Physical and spiritual healings are no
problem for him. Anyone who disagrees doesn't know Jesus
very well. Continue to ask and believe.

Jesus, I believe in your power to perform miracles. I will
spend more time focusing on you and less time listening
to those who tell me that trusting you is not realistic.

OCTOBER 2

Anxiety in a man's heart weighs him down, but a good word makes him glad. (Proverbs 12:25)

My wife is an amazing person. She always seems to know what to say to me when I am struggling. There have been many occasions when I've been overwhelmed with various issues and at just the opportune time Eileen offered some advice or encouragement that gave me hope. I am blessed to have her in my life.

Even if you struggle with anxiety, you can help others by offering a kind word or listening as they discuss their problems. Sometimes it doesn't even matter what you say; your presence and willingness to listen is enough. In addition, helping others with their problems is a great way to get your mind off your own worries. Jesus often comforts us by sending the right person at the right time. Why not let yourself be that person?

God, please use me to reassure those who are anxious and worried the way others have often encouraged me.

OCTOBER 3

It is the Lord who goes before you; he will be
with you, he will not fail you or forsake you; do
not fear or be dismayed. (Deuteronomy 31:8)

Forgetting about God and his assistance is a very common
problem. It was also a problem in Moses' day. As he prepared
to turn over his leadership role to Joshua, Moses wanted to
be sure that the Israelites and their new leader would always
remember God's involvement in their lives.

Every day we face challenges that can cause us to become
overwhelmed. Unless we work at it, we can easily lose sight
of God's presence. He is always beside us, ready and willing to help with anything that comes our way. Have no fear.
With God by your side, you are never alone.

*Keep me mindful of your presence in my life,
Father. Knowing that you are with me wherever
I go is the remedy for fear and dismay.*

OCTOBER 4

And he said to all, "If any man would come after me, let him deny himself and take up his cross daily and follow me." (Luke 9:23)

Are you a follower of Christ? How can you be sure? In this challenging verse Jesus lays out the criteria for those who truly desire to follow him. And while Matthew and Mark both record Christ's words on this matter (see Matthew 16:24; Mark 8:34), Luke raises the bar by adding one word: *daily*.

If you and I desire to follow Christ, we must take up our cross not yearly, not monthly, not weekly—but daily. While on this earth we will encounter some form of suffering on a regular basis. It may be minor or it may be major, but it will be there. Rather than viewing suffering as a curse, look at it as an opportunity to grow closer to Jesus. When you carry your cross daily, you are walking in Christ's footsteps and sharing his mission. What an honor!

Jesus, I offer up all my suffering and ask you to use it in the best way possible. Show me ways I can deny myself and carry my cross.

OCTOBER 5

Every good endowment and every perfect
gift is from above, coming down from the
Father of lights with whom there is no variation
or shadow due to change. (James 1:17)

I always get a special feeling when I visit stores, restaurants, and bakeries that were a part of my youth. With all the changes we experience in life, it's comforting to know that some things remain the same. The ultimate example of this can be found in almighty God, who never, ever changes.

Even though I may be riding on an emotional roller coaster, I can count on the fact that God never changes. My prayers will never go unanswered because he is too busy or in a bad mood. He is never surprised by anything that happens or overwhelmed when complications arise in my life. He provides stability in a very unstable world.

Thank you for never changing, God. When the
world seems out of control, it's such a source of
strength in my life to know you remain the same.

OCTOBER 6

Even though I walk through the valley of the shadow of death, I fear no evil; for you are with me; your rod and your staff they comfort me. (Psalm 23:4)

I don't have the greatest memory in the world, but there are several Bible verses I have been able to memorize. Generally they are the ones I turn to over and over again. Psalm 23:4 is one of those verses. Its message can comfort every anxious person.

We often feel like we are walking through the valley of the shadow of death, but this verse reminds us that we are never alone. As long as Jesus is beside me, nothing can harm me. This verse doesn't attempt to sugarcoat the difficulties we face. Life definitely has its challenges, but God doesn't ask us to face them alone. He is always with us.

I know I will continue to face challenges
in life, Jesus, but I take comfort in the fact
that you and I will face them together.

OCTOBER 7

So Gideon took ten men of his servants, and did as the Lord had told him; but because he was too afraid of his family and the men of the town to do it by day, he did it by night. (Judges 6:27)

When instructed by God to tear down the altar his father had built to worship the false god Baal, Gideon obeyed. But because he was afraid of potential repercussions, he did it at night. While one could make the case that Gideon was cowardly, I think it took great courage to do what he did.

When stepping out in faith, there is something to be said for taking baby steps. God understands that faith grows gradually, and he doesn't expect us to learn to trust him overnight. What he does expect, however, is that we make an attempt to exercise our faith each day. When we ask for what we need and learn to step out of our comfort zones when necessary, our confidence in him will grow. How can you trust God more today? Start taking those baby steps and you'll soon be leaping!

Father, show me ways to trust you more today than I did yesterday. Step by step, I will exercise my faith on a regular basis.

OCTOBER 8

"And behold, I am with you always, to the close of the age." (Matthew 28:20)

I learned to drive when I was a junior in high school. Although I couldn't wait to begin driving, major highways intimidated me. When I first ventured out on a busy street, I was happy to be accompanied by my driving instructor. As an added measure of protection, the car was equipped with a passenger's side steering wheel and brake pedal. Knowing that I had a security blanket took away much of my anxiety.

Think of how difficult life would be if you didn't have any faith—if you didn't sense God's presence at all. Many people today don't have faith, and we see the devastating results in their lives. Even though we face challenges and obstacles, we have the assurance that God will always remain with us. With him we can do all things and we can face all things.

I am grateful for my faith in you, Jesus. With you by my side, I can face any challenge, and no obstacle is insurmountable.

OCTOBER 9

"Fear not, for I have redeemed you; I have called
you by name, you are mine." (Isaiah 43:1)

Did you ever have a chance to meet a celebrity? If so, did
he or she call you by name? When it happened to me, I was
thrilled that a famous person would actually use my name
when addressing me. It made me feel important.

The thought of God calling me by name boggles my
mind, but that is exactly what he does. He knows each of
us intimately and refers to us by name. What is even more
incredible is that he pursues a relationship with us. Even
though I ignored him for many years, he never stopped
knocking on my door. Nothing can ever make me feel better than reflecting on the fact that the Lord of the universe
wants to be my friend.

*The fact that you know my name makes me
feel very special, God. Thank you for loving me
so much and never forgetting about me.*

OCTOBER 10

"You have sown much, and harvested little; you eat, but you never have enough; you drink, but you never have your fill; you clothe yourselves, but no one is warm." (Haggai 1:6)

God's words to the prophet Haggai leave little to the imagination. Clearly he was warning the people about the danger of seeking happiness in material things. Despite his admonishment, however, today people are more materialistic than ever. Even sadder is the fact that you and I fall into this trap.

While it's not necessarily sinful, when we seek happiness in the things of the world, we forget that lasting peace can only come from Christ. Instead we spend countless hours pursuing fleeting pleasures that bring only momentary happiness. Having a personal relationship with Christ has brought me more joy than all my possessions combined. Growing in faith requires work, but it is absolutely worth it. Make the decision to turn to God each day by praying, reading the Bible, and spending time in his presence. You'll soon discover that he will fulfill all of your needs.

Only you can satisfy my needs, Jesus.
Teach me to see through the false sense of
fulfillment the world around me promises.

OCTOBER 11

Rejoice in your hope, be patient in tribulation,
be constant in prayer. (Romans 12:12)

If you're having a bad day, I don't think it would be possible for me to give you better advice than what St. Paul expresses in this verse. In one sentence you have everything you need to deal with any problem that arises in your life.

With Jesus there is always hope. But what about those times when all seems hopeless? Being patient in tribulation is also hard to accept. How can we learn to be patient when dealing with extended periods of suffering? The secret to this entire verse lies in the last clause. By praying daily we will receive the grace to be patient and the hope to believe that everything will ultimately work out for the best. It's then that we will find it possible to rejoice at all times.

God, I know that frequent prayer makes a huge difference in my life. Thank you for giving me the key to stay hopeful and patient, even when I experience trials.

OCTOBER 12

You also be patient. Establish your hearts, for the coming of the Lord is at hand. (James 5:8)

St. James obviously recognized that people have a tendency to lose patience during extended periods of suffering. As a result, he included this important reminder in his letter. Just as "the farmer waits for the precious fruit of the earth" (see James 5:7), we are encouraged to be patient with the difficulties we face, knowing that a bright future lies ahead.

We don't hear enough about the virtue of hope. Hope gives us the ability to rise above the challenges of life. This powerful virtue, received at baptism, allows us to hang in there and believe that God really does know what he's doing. Although we may not be able to see it now, one day everything will make sense.

God, please increase my hope and show me how
every challenge I face will benefit me in some way.
I want my heart to be firmly established in you.

OCTOBER 13

"Come to me, all who labor and are heavy laden,
and I will give you rest." (Matthew 11:28)

In 1997 Eileen and I dealt with one of our greatest challenges: the very real possibility that our twin daughters would not be born alive. After an especially discouraging visit with the perinatal doctors at Our Lady of Lourdes Hospital, we knelt before Jesus in the hospital chapel, where I saw this verse above the sanctuary. I immediately felt a sense of peace.

There is never a reason for us to carry our crosses alone. If we allow ourselves to become stressed and fail to turn to Jesus, it is our fault. He is always there, ready to give us the rest that we need. If you feel overwhelmed, turn to him today and receive the peace that he wants you to have.

Thank you for inviting me to come to you, Jesus. When my heart is heavy, I need the rest that only you can give.

OCTOBER 14

For he who sanctifies and those who
are sanctified have all one origin.
That is why he is not ashamed to call
them brethren. (Hebrews 2:11)

Isn't it great to know that Jesus is your brother? Because of his willingness to take on human flesh, we have been blessed with the privilege of entering into an incredible family. With God as our Father, Jesus as our brother, and Mary as our mother, we can't possibly lose. Their support enables us to handle anything that comes our way.

In spite of this we still find ourselves dejected and worried when things don't go our way. We lose sight of the fact that we are members of a heavenly family. Make it a point to reflect on how wonderful it is to have access to such powerful heavenly allies. And while you're at it, reach out to your brother Jesus. He wants to help you with your struggles and share all your joys.

Thank you for being my brother, Jesus. It's a great honor to be a part of your family.

OCTOBER 15

"Call to me and I will answer you, and will tell you great and hidden things which you have not known." (Jeremiah 33:3)

We often fail to ask God for what we need, which is tragic because he is always ready to answer our prayers and often comes through in ways that we would never have thought possible. When I think back over how he has answered my prayers, I am astonished to realize that he has far exceeded my expectations.

As soon as you finish reading this meditation, I urge you to turn to Jesus and ask for what you need. And don't hold back! Ask for that one request that seems impossible to you. Give God a chance to show you what he can do in your life. Ask him for what you need and keep asking. It might take some time, but you will eventually receive an answer. I have learned from experience that his answer may blow you away!

When I call, you promise to answer, God.
Whether I need wisdom regarding a decision,
healing for an old wound, or help with a tough
relationship, I will present you with my greatest
needs today and eagerly await your response.

OCTOBER 16

"Yet he is not far from each one of us." (Acts 17:27)

When I was a child I would often go shopping with my mother. One day we were in a department store and I began hiding in the racks of clothes. I did such a good job that one of my greatest fears came true—I became separated from my mother! When I realized that I was lost, I started to cry. Eventually a salesperson found me and took me to the store's office, where I was reunited with my mother. Although my story had a happy ending and happened fifty years ago, I can still feel the terror I experienced when I realized that my mother wasn't nearby.

You might feel like you're lost on a remote island and God is nowhere to be found, but as St. Paul observes in this verse, God is never far from you. Even if you don't sense his presence, he is there. Keeping that in mind should make you feel very secure.

Whenever I begin to feel afraid, Jesus, I will remember that you are near.

OCTOBER 17

The Lord is my light and my salvation; whom
shall I fear? The Lord is the stronghold of my
life; of whom shall I be afraid? (Psalm 27:1)

If Jesus truly is my light and my salvation, why would I ever be afraid? This is a great question—one we should ask ourselves often. If we truly believe that God will provide for all of our needs and make it possible for us to live with him in heaven, why should anything frighten us?

In all honesty we don't think about God's goodness as much as we should. As a result, we forget that he would never desert us in our time of need. Problems arise, we become distracted, and we forget that God is still in charge. So what's the solution? Reading this verse is a great place to start. After you answer both of these questions with a resounding "NO-BODY," you'll be able to regain your focus and confidence.

*God, with you I have all that I need. When I
reflect on who you are in my life, I can see that
there really is no reason to be afraid. Faith in you
allows me to live confidently and fearlessly.*

OCTOBER 18

And Simon answered, "Master, we toiled all
night and took nothing! But at your word
I will let down the nets." (Luke 5:5)

As a fisherman by trade, Simon knew a thing or two about
catching fish. And after an unproductive night on the seas,
one wouldn't expect him to be receptive to advice from a
non-fisherman . . . but he was. When Jesus instructed him to
put out into the deep and lower his nets, Simon obeyed. As
a result he and his fellow fishermen caught so many fish that
their boats began to sink.

Regardless of how much our culture values indepen-
dence and personal autonomy, the reality is that total self-re-
liance is both frustrating and ineffective. Failing to seek
God's assistance with our daily responsibilities only leads to
anxiety and lack of success. Just as he helped Simon, Jesus
will help you. Just make sure you don't become so proud
that you think you don't need his help. You do.

I will seek your help with all my responsibilities,
Lord. I know you won't let me down.

OCTOBER 19

I form light and create darkness, I make
well-being and create woe, I am the Lord,
who do all these things. (Isaiah 45:7)

When something pleasant happens, it is easy to give thanks to God. On the other hand, very few individuals react naturally with gratitude when pain and suffering comes along. We might even be tempted to believe that some events are out of God's control. As this verse illustrates, however, *everything* that happens comes from God.

Although God never wills evil actions, he certainly allows them to happen—and he can bring good out of them. Remembering this will bring you great peace when you face something devastating. If something unpleasant happens to you today, view it as coming from God's hand and know that it is somehow designed to benefit you. Make it a habit to give thanks for the difficulties you encounter. The end result will be that your happiness and well-being will no longer be dependent on the weather, financial success, or good health. Your demeanor will be one of joyful confidence and trust.

God, help me to recognize that everything
that happens to me today comes from you
and is designed to benefit me spiritually.

OCTOBER 20

"So it was not you who sent me here, but God; and he has made me a father to Pharaoh, and lord of all his house and ruler over all the land of Egypt." (Genesis 45:8)

When my father was suffering from cancer in 2002, my Aunt Florence and Uncle Walt wanted to cheer him up with a visit. As they sat in my parents' living room, chatting, my father suddenly slumped over in his chair. My aunt and uncle took charge, called the ambulance, and stayed with my mother (who was in the early stages of dementia) at the hospital until my sister and I arrived. My father died on the way to the hospital, and it's a blessing that they were there for my mother.

When Joseph was sold into slavery, he didn't know at the time that it was an act of divine providence, but it certainly was. Because of his rise to power in Egypt, Joseph was responsible for storing up much-needed grain that would preserve the life of his family during the famine. If you get the feeling that God is asking you to do something, don't ignore it. He often places us where we're needed, even if we don't understand the big picture.

God, I am open to doing your will today.
Please use me where I'm needed the most.

OCTOBER 21

But he said to them, "It is I; do
not be afraid." (John 6:20)

For many people—perhaps even most of us—feeling afraid is an everyday occurrence. Our level of fear may increase or decrease, but if we're honest, it's rare to make it through an entire day without being afraid of something. Even though Jesus first spoke these words two thousand years ago, they are just as relevant for us today. Jesus is with us, and he doesn't want us to be afraid.

There is no crisis too big for Jesus to handle. Take his words to heart and remember that it is possible to live without fear. It will only happen, however, if you stay close to him. Trying to make it through this life without Jesus is a frightening proposition, but we don't have to worry about that. He is with us and can help us to live each day confidently, no matter what happens. Do not be afraid!

Thank you for reassuring me of your protection,
Jesus. When I am tempted to be afraid, I
will remember that you are with me!

OCTOBER 22

He heals the brokenhearted, and binds
up their wounds. (Psalm 147:3)

Many of Jesus' miracles involve physical ailments. We know
that he can give sight to the blind and hearing to the deaf.
We also know that he can raise people from the dead. What
we sometimes forget is that he can bring healing to the
brokenhearted.

People can hurt us in many ways. The betrayal of a
friend or the disappointment of rejection can be just as
painful as any physical ailment. Jesus knows what you are
going through, as he experienced a great deal of rejection
and betrayal. He is a true friend and can heal your broken
heart. Reach out to him and ask for healing.

Jesus, you understand those who are brokenhearted.
Please comfort me in my time of emotional distress.

OCTOBER 23

All Scripture is inspired by God and profitable for teaching, for reproof, for correction, and for training in righteousness. (2 Timothy 3:16)

The Bible is no ordinary book. The Church teaches that within its pages God the Father meets us and speaks with us. Therefore you can be assured that God speaks to you when you read the Bible. What a great blessing!

Take advantage of this great gift and spend some time reading the Bible today. I have tried many remedies for anxiety, and daily Scripture reading is one of the best. When you read the Bible, you're not just reading a book . . . you're having an encounter with God!

God, thank you for speaking to me through the Bible. It's great to hear your voice!

OCTOBER 24

In every place incense is offered to my name, and a pure offering; for my name is great among the nations, says the Lord of hosts. (Malachi 1:11)

If you have ever experienced the feeling of hopelessness, you know just how painful it can be. However, no situation is truly hopeless. With God all things are possible. The greatest challenge we face is being able to cling to hope when all looks bleak.

Here is something to remember: The most important activity you can ever engage in on earth is participating in the Holy Mass. In addition to providing an abundance of graces, attending Mass will fill your heart with peace. Several years ago I made the decision to attend daily Mass, and it has changed my life. If you are feeling hopeless, bring your intentions to the Mass and hand them over to Jesus. And don't forget, there is always hope.

Thank you for the gift of the Mass, Jesus. Please increase my appreciation of its power. When I'm feeling hopeless, participating in the liturgy will lift my spirits and take away my worry.

OCTOBER 25

Weeping may last for the night, but joy comes in the morning. (Psalm 30:5)

I have experienced many emotional ups and downs in my life. As time goes by, however, I have learned that these highs and lows are just part of life. While I don't like feeling down, I now realize that I will eventually feel better. As a result I am able to ride out the storm and avoid panicking.

If you are struggling now, take comfort in the fact that better days are ahead. Reading the Bible, praying, and receiving the sacraments can help you to experience peace while you wait. Sometimes getting a good night's sleep can even make your situation look brighter. Just as the rain will eventually give way to sunshine, your problems will eventually pass.

God, this life is a series of highs and lows. Thank you for being my shelter until the storms subside.

OCTOBER 26

And when the Lord saw her, he had
compassion on her and said to her,
"Do not weep." (Luke 7:13)

When Jesus encountered a widow whose only son had just died, he was moved. Telling her not to weep, he proceeded to raise the man from the dead. And while the act of raising the dead generally gets the most attention in this episode, I am drawn to the fact that Jesus was compassionate.

When we are struggling, it's always good to know that someone cares. It can make even the most difficult suffering bearable. This incident reminds us that we never struggle alone. If you are suffering, Jesus feels your pain and wants to restore your peace. Ask him to help you, and trust him to do whatever it takes to assist you.

Thank you for having compassion on me, Jesus.
It is a great comfort to know that you care.

OCTOBER 27

But Moses said to the Lord, "Oh, my Lord, I
am not eloquent, either heretofore or since
you have spoken to your servant; but I am slow
of speech and of tongue." (Exodus 4:10)

Have you ever felt that God was calling you to do something,
but you dismissed the idea because you thought you weren't
good enough? If so, you and Moses have something in common! When asked by God to lead the Israelites out of slavery
in Egypt, Moses declined because he lacked speaking skills.
By responding the way he did, he totally ignored an important fact: God will never ask us to do anything without providing the assistance that we need.

Why is it so easy to forget this basic fact? More often
than not it's because of pride. We can become so used to
thinking that we are responsible for our success that we forget to ask God for help. If you feel God is asking you to do
something challenging, turn to him for help. With God's assistance I have been able to do things that I never imagined
were possible.

*Jesus, help me to remember that you will assist
me with any assignment that you give me.*

OCTOBER 28

The Lord opened her heart to listen to
what was said by Paul. (Acts 16:14)

Even if you have the best of intentions, sharing your faith
can be frustrating. It can be a challenge to keep your cool,
especially when your attempt to share the Good News is met
with anger or ridicule. Here's something to help you remain
calm even when it appears that your efforts are bearing no
fruit: You're not really the one doing the work. No matter
how persuasive you might be, no conversion ever takes place
without the gift of grace.

While traveling through Philippi St. Paul encountered a
woman named Lydia. Because God opened her heart, she was
willing to listen to Paul's message and be baptized. We should
always pray before, during, and after we share the gospel with
others. In addition to the obvious benefits, this helps us to remember that we are just planting seeds. God is responsible
for the end result. Knowing that will make it easier to respond
calmly, no matter how much resistance you meet.

God, open the hearts of all those I will share my faith with
today. Prepare them to receive your message with joy, and if
they don't at first, teach me to respond with compassion.

OCTOBER 29

How lovely is your dwelling place,
O Lord of hosts! (Psalm 84:1)

When overcome by stress, many individuals have a "happy place" they like to visit. Sometimes the trip takes place in one's mind, and other times it involves an actual destination. I've had many such places in my life, but nothing comes close to providing the peace I feel when I'm in the presence of God.

Reading the Bible or praying always brings me some level of peace, but paying a visit to Jesus in a church or adoration chapel is my ultimate source of comfort. When I sit before Jesus, fully present in the Blessed Sacrament, my cares fade away. Being in his presence is very powerful.

Rather than take my word for it, try it yourself and see what happens. Start with ten or fifteen minutes one or two times a week. If you're not sure what to say, sit quietly and meditate on the fact that you are sitting before the Lord of the universe. If you feel like talking, tell him your concerns. I predict that you will soon be looking for ways to spend more time with him.

It is wonderful to be in your presence, Jesus. No matter how stressful life can get, sitting quietly before you puts things in perspective.

OCTOBER 30

Now I rejoice in my sufferings for your sake, and in my flesh I complete what is lacking in Christ's afflictions for the sake of his body, that is, the Church. (Colossians 1:24)

Many of the statements made by St. Paul are nothing short of shocking. In my opinion this one may be the most startling of them all. How could he possibly rejoice in his suffering, and how could Christ's sacrifice be incomplete?

Paul was in no way insinuating that the sacrifice of Jesus on the cross was incomplete. Christ did exactly what was required to redeem us. As members of the mystical body of Christ (the Church), however, you and I have been given the privilege of helping him with his mission, and one of the ways we do this is by offering up our sufferings. Paul understands the value of suffering. He rejoices not because he enjoys the pain, but because he knows he is helping Jesus.

Thank you for the privilege of assisting you, Jesus. I give you all my sufferings, and I ask you to use them as you see fit.

OCTOBER 31

He who gives heed to the word will prosper, and happy is he who trusts in the Lord. (Proverbs 16:20)

Can you imagine how happy you would be if you had complete trust in God? Don't stress about getting there, but picture yourself trusting him completely. What might that look like? For one thing you would be content with anything that happened in your life, pleasant or unpleasant, because you would be confident that he knows what is best for you.

So how do we get to a place of total trust? How can we develop the confidence that God always knows best and will supply all our needs? It starts by accepting that we can't force ourselves to trust him. I have tried it many times, and it simply doesn't work. The most effective approach is to begin by admitting the obvious—tell God you are afraid to trust him. You can be brutally honest—he knows anyway! Next make an effort to know him better (through prayer, Bible reading, and the sacraments) and ask for help. Keep working at it and see what happens. I'm confident you'll be pleased with the results.

Jesus, I have to admit that I don't trust you at times. Whenever my worries threaten to overwhelm me, please help me to believe that you know what's best for me.

NOVEMBER 1

Therefore, since we are surrounded by so great a
cloud of witnesses . . . let us run with perseverance
the race that is set before us. (Hebrews 12:1)

Some days I don't feel very saintly. In fact that happens a lot.
Even though my mind knows I was created for holiness, my
heart struggles to believe it. The Church helps us by giving
us the solemnity of All Saints' Day. It is a day set aside to
celebrate all the saints in heaven, and it serves as a reminder
that sanctity is within our reach.

You and I were created to be saints. The fact that we don't
feel like saints doesn't change anything. If you get into the
habit of reading the lives of the saints, you will be surprised
to discover that they didn't always walk around with their
hands folded in prayer and halos over their heads. The saints
had weaknesses, just like we do. Do you want to be a saint? If
your answer is yes, you're on the right track. Ask God to give
you the grace you need, and take it one day at a time!

*God, I certainly don't feel like a saint. But you
call me to be one. Give me the desire to cooperate
with your grace and grow in holiness.*

NOVEMBER 2

He will wipe away every tear from their eyes, and death shall be no more, neither shall there be mourning nor crying nor pain any more, for the former things have passed away. (Revelation 21:4)

Death can be a frightening concept, because most of us fear the unknown. In addition to worrying about what will happen to us when we die, we might worry about our deceased relatives and friends. We wish we could do something to help them. We can. Today the Church remembers the souls who are suffering in purgatory. On All Souls' Day we are encouraged to pray for those who have died. By doing so we can help them tremendously.

In addition to the souls of our deceased loved ones, there are many other souls who need our prayers. Since many non-Catholic Christians don't believe in praying for the dead, there are millions of souls who are not being prayed for. Your prayers may be responsible for helping them experience the joy of heaven. It is an awesome privilege to pray for the dead.

May the souls of the faithful departed, through the mercy of God, rest in peace. Amen.

NOVEMBER 3

I have learned, in whatever state I am,
to be content. (Philippians 4:11)

Many of us are searching for that "one thing" that will bring us happiness. It may be more money, a new job, a physical healing, more friends, a vacation, or any number of other things. Whatever it is, we become convinced that this need is all that is standing between us and happiness. Unfortunately, when we find that one thing, we generally begin to pursue something else.

Writing to the Philippians from prison, St. Paul revealed that learning to be content is the secret to happiness. But how can we be content when we want so many things? It starts by recognizing that if we have God in our lives, we have all we need. He has redeemed us and opened the gates of heaven. Anything else is just icing on the cake!

When I have you in my life, God, I have
all that I need. I am thankful that I can be
content with the way things are right now.

NOVEMBER 4

God thunders wondrously with his voice, he does great things which we cannot comprehend. (Job 37:5)

I don't need to know how a car engine operates in order to drive to the store. It's not necessary to understand computer technology to browse the Internet. If we stop and think about it, every day we make use of devices without fully grasping how they operate. Why is it that we feel we must understand all of God's actions?

Because our human intelligence is limited, we will never be able to fully understand God's reasoning. Rather than becoming frustrated with our inability to do so, there's plenty about God that we can understand. He constantly expresses his love for us through the events that occur in our lives, and he's promised to walk with us along life's journey. That really is all we need to know.

God, it's a relief to not question your every action but instead to trust and obey. Thank you for showing your love to me in so many ways that I can understand.

NOVEMBER 5

Jesus Christ is the same yesterday,
today and for ever. (Hebrews 13:8)

I strongly recommend that you get into the habit of reading the Gospels each day. Ten or fifteen minutes of reflecting on the life of Christ is definitely time well spent. But don't view it as a history lesson. As this verse from Hebrews reminds us, Jesus Christ is the same today as he was two thousand years ago. Anything he did then he can still do today.

Do you have a pressing problem weighing you down? Are you anxious about a particular situation? Imagine how you might have handled these issues if you lived during the time of Christ. Think about how comforting it would have been to know that he was available to listen to you and handle all of your problems. Jesus hasn't changed. He performed miracles in the past and can do so today. The only thing that stops him is our failure to ask.

Jesus, in the face of so much instability and
change, I'm grateful that you never change.
Teach me to focus on spiritual realities instead of
on the uncertain circumstances around me.

NOVEMBER 6

After these things God tested Abraham,
and said to him, "Abraham!" And he
said, "Here am I." (Genesis 22:1)

Sometimes we like to create our own version of God. We decide how he will act and what he will say. Aside from the fact that it isn't based in reality, this practice can be spiritually dangerous. While we should all seek to know God, we want to know him as he really is and not as we think he should be.

The idea of being tested is not very appealing, is it? In particular I don't like the thought of being tested by God. This verse clearly states that it does happen, however. God didn't test Abraham to learn how he would respond (he already knew that), but to help him grow in faith. Make no mistake about it—God will test you, too. You will experience events in your life that will give you the opportunity to trust God even when you're scared to death. How will you respond?

> *Father, teach me to trust you—even when I*
> *am afraid. And teach me to see you as you*
> *really are, not how I'd like you to be.*

NOVEMBER 7

"Never since the world began has it been heard that any one opened the eyes of a man born blind." (John 9:32)

We often look to history to predict the future. If something has never happened in the past, we assume that it won't happen in the future. If we apply the same logic to God, however, we do him a disservice. It doesn't matter if there is a precedent or not—he can do all things!

After his eyesight was restored by Jesus, the man born blind acknowledged the monumental nature of his healing. The Bible is filled with stories of God doing the impossible. In the past you may not have been able to overcome a sinful habit, pray regularly, or stop worrying, but that doesn't mean it can't happen in the future. Jesus can do all things, and you can overcome great obstacles through him.

Jesus, I become discouraged when I look at the many times I have failed in the past. Grant me the hope that I need to face the future with confidence, knowing that you can do all things.

NOVEMBER 8

Yes, you light my lamp; the Lord my God
lightens my darkness. (Psalm 18:28)

When I began to sense God calling me to full-time ministry several years ago, I struggled to discern his will. It was a difficult process at first, but it grew easier over time. Although I still have to work at it, I now feel confident that I can determine what he is calling me to do. The key is to make use of the light provided by his presence.

Walking by faith is not the same thing as walking in the darkness. As long as we stay close to Jesus, we will always have his light to guide us. Through prayer, the teachings of the Church, the Bible, and the sacraments, we have all the light we need to see where we are going and to make decisions that please God.

You light my path, Jesus. Continue to guide
my decisions every day of my life.

NOVEMBER 9

God chose the foolish in the world to shame
the wise, God chose what is weak in the world
to shame the strong. (1 Corinthians 1:27)

I am not a very likely person to be working as a full-time speaker and author. I have a business degree, I've always had a fear of public speaking, and I never enjoyed writing. If you throw in the fact that I was a very lukewarm Catholic for most of my life, it is astonishing to think that I now make my living as an evangelist. But as crazy as it seems, God called me to work for him, and I'm grateful that he did!

As can be seen throughout history, God chooses unlikely individuals to do his work. The main quality he looks for is a willingness to serve him. Are you open to working for Jesus in some way? He has a job for you. Don't be afraid that you're not qualified. If he calls and you say yes, I can vouch for the fact that he will provide on-the-job training!

Jesus, please use me to advance your kingdom
on earth. I will trust you to provide me
with the skills I need to serve you.

NOVEMBER 10

In the day of prosperity be joyful, and in the day of adversity consider; God has made the one as well as the other, so that man may not find out anything that will be after him. (Ecclesiastes 7:14)

I often wish I could predict the future. On the other hand, if we knew ahead of time that suffering was headed our way, we would find it difficult to enjoy the serenity of the present moment. All things considered, God once again knows best. By not revealing the future to us, he helps us to focus on today.

If there are no major problems in your life, be glad! If you are struggling, know that there is a reason, offer up your suffering, and take comfort in the fact that it won't last forever. Finally, don't waste time worrying about what may happen in the future. Deal with the issues you are facing today. God wants you to live fully in the present; each day has its own gifts.

Father, teach me to live one day at a time,
knowing the future is safe in your hands.

NOVEMBER 11

But the Lord is faithful; he will strengthen you
and guard you from evil. (2 Thessalonians 3:3)

Evil is such a nasty word, isn't it? It's typically one that we
use for the actions of criminals and immoral people. I don't
know about you, but I get very uncomfortable using that
word when describing my own behavior. Like it or not, however, every time we sin we are committing an evil action.

As threatening as the temptation to sin is, however, we
are not helpless. God provides us with the grace that we need
in order to avoid falling into the trap of the evil one. I have
discovered that the sacrament of confession is a great source
of protection for me. In addition to being absolved of my
sins, I receive the sacramental grace needed to protect me
from sinning in the future. While I am far from perfect, I
am making progress, and you can, too. Frequent confession
will change your life. Try going at least monthly for several
months and see what happens.

*Thank you for protecting me from evil, God, and
for the sacrament of confession. Even if I feel some
resistance, I will go to confession frequently.*

NOVEMBER 12

"He is the living God, enduring for ever; his kingdom shall never be destroyed, and his dominion shall be to the end." (Daniel 6:26)

Judging by this excerpt from his decree to the people, King Darius had a good understanding of God's power. We would be wise to take his proclamation seriously, as it reminds us that we are in good hands. Even when it seems like we may be losing the battle in today's crazy world, it is just an illusion. God is in charge, and his kingdom will have no end.

Each day you must make a choice. You can choose to saturate your mind with the news of violent crime, corruption, terrorism, and materialism proclaimed in the media, or you can turn to the inspired Word of God in sacred Scripture. You can probably guess which option will bring you greater peace. Don't listen to the naysayers. God is bigger than the world's problems. Don't lose hope!

Thy kingdom come, thy will be done
on earth as it is in heaven.

NOVEMBER 13

But Jesus came and touched them, saying,
"Rise, and have no fear." (Matthew 17:7)

When Jesus appeared in his glorified state before Peter, James, and John it must have been an impressive sight. So much so, in fact, that Peter wanted to stay on the mountain (see Matthew 17:4). That was not possible. When it was time to leave, Jesus reassured his followers with these words.

When you are facing uncertainty, getting out of bed in the morning can be difficult. In an effort to feel secure, we sometimes wish that we could hide from our problems. God doesn't want us to do that. Instead he wants us to listen to his words and take them to heart. If you have Jesus in your life, there is no need to be afraid.

Thank you for your reassurance, Jesus. With you by my side, I know I can face any problem that comes my way.

NOVEMBER 14

For I know the plans I have for you, says the Lord, plans for welfare and not for evil, to give you a future and a hope. (Jeremiah 29:11)

Guess what? God knows everything that will happen to you in the future. Even though you and I are surprised by events every day, they are all part of his plan. Want some even better news? It's all good!

God does indeed have great plans for you. His desire is that you become a saint. He knows that being holy is the way to be truly happy. And while that may seem like an unreachable goal, it is totally realistic. Everything that happens to you today (and for the rest of your life) is part of God's plan to transform you and help you get to heaven. Keep this in mind, ask for the strength to deal with the challenges you face, and get excited. Heaven will be awesome!

Even though I don't know what lies ahead, God, I know that you do. Help me to trust you with today and with all that my future holds. Thank you for showing me how to be fulfilled here on earth and in heaven.

NOVEMBER 15

Rejoice always, pray constantly, give thanks in all circumstances; for this is the will of God in Christ Jesus for you. (1 Thessalonians 5:16–18)

It's not always easy knowing God's will, is it? Here is the answer, direct from St. Paul! And if you are looking for a Bible passage to post on your refrigerator or bathroom mirror, this is an excellent choice. This message, although simple to understand, can be difficult to put into practice. Why? Because on an average day, you aren't going to feel like doing any of these three things!

Following God's will—which is guaranteed to bring peace—sometimes requires us to do things that we don't want to do. Giving thanks, rejoicing, and praying are all acts of the will. You can choose to do them, even when you'd rather not. Don't dismiss St. Paul's advice because it involves too much effort. Instead make these steps a part of your daily routine and enjoy the peace that results!

Jesus, today I will find something to be joyful about, I'll make time to pray, and I'll thank you for something that I've been complaining about.

NOVEMBER 16

But he did not answer her a
word. (Matthew 15:23)

We all experience times when Jesus is silent. I can handle it
once or twice, but after weeks or months of praying with
no answer, I start to get annoyed. Yet I have learned that the
worst thing I can do when this happens is to stop praying.
Even if I feel like I'm being a pest, I keep asking God for what
I need—and so should you. The fact that he is silent doesn't
mean he isn't listening or is saying no.

When the Canaanite woman approached Jesus and asked
him to heal her daughter, her request was met with silence.
And while that might deter many of us, it didn't stop the
woman from persisting. She didn't even stop asking when
Jesus referred to her as a dog (see Matthew 15:26). Instead she
knelt before him, begging for her daughter to be healed. And
guess what happened. Her request was granted because of
her great faith. So if Jesus doesn't appear to respond to your
prayer requests, keep asking . . . and asking . . . and asking.

*Jesus, I will not take your silence to be a
rejection of my prayers. Just like the Canaanite
woman, I will keep asking for what I need.*

NOVEMBER 17

And they went away in the boat to a lonely place by themselves. (Mark 6:32)

Sometimes life can seem like one distraction after another. Between our scheduled plans and the disruptions that arise, focusing on spiritual matters can be very difficult. How can you possibly find time to pray if there aren't enough hours in the day to do things that *have to* get done?

By retreating with his apostles to a "lonely place," Jesus emphasized the need for taking a break. As someone who is self-employed, I struggle with the idea of retreating from my duties. I have learned, though, that it is necessary—and beneficial. Taking time for prayer or spiritual reading will give you the strength you need to handle your daily work. Don't ignore it. If Jesus made it a point to get away and take a break, you can, too.

Instead of seeing my prayer time as just another task to check off my list, Jesus, today I I will see it as a time to relax and recharge with a good friend—you!

NOVEMBER 18

"Yet you say, 'The way of the Lord is not just.' Hear now, O house of Israel: Is my way not just? Is it not your ways that are not just?" (Ezekiel 18:25)

It's easy to blame God for the misfortune in our lives. I have done it many times and I'm sure you have, too. When I consider God's question to the Israelites (through the prophet Ezekiel), however, I become speechless and realize how self-centered I can be. I don't have a good answer for him. Do you?

Blaming God (and others) for your misfortune is the best way to ensure that you will be miserable. Aside from that, it isn't fair to God. Everything that happens to us is an expression of his love. When I was a child I didn't think it was fair that my parents took me to the doctor's office for booster shots or sent me to my room when I disobeyed. Now, of course, I understand that these unpleasant actions were performed out of love. Don't blame God when things don't go your way. Everything he does illustrates just how much he loves you.

God, sometimes I treat you unfairly by questioning
your actions in my life. I'm sorry. I know you
love me and only want the best for me.

NOVEMBER 19

"For this is the will of my Father, that every one who sees the Son and believes in him should have eternal life; and I will raise him up at the last day." (John 6:40)

We might not see the big picture, especially when we are struggling with a major problem. Often our only desire is for the problem to go away. When we feel miserable, we want to be happy . . . NOW!

God wants us to be happy, too, but he loves us too much to allow our joy to be momentary. He wants it to last forever. That eternal happiness can be found in heaven, and he has reserved a place for you there. Sometimes, however, it is necessary to endure short-term suffering in this life in order to experience lasting happiness in heaven. Don't lose sight of the big picture. Stay close to Jesus. He wants you to be happy not just today, but forever.

God, I'm grateful that you don't want me to settle for a shallow joy that won't last. When I'm tempted to demand instant gratification, give me the grace to see the big picture.

NOVEMBER 20

"And I will make of you a great nation, and I will bless you, and make your name great, so that you will be a blessing." (Genesis 12:2)

On the surface God's promise to the seventy-five-year-old Abram seems a bit far-fetched. But Abram believed and obeyed the Lord. He left his homeland and trusted God. In the end everything that God promised did indeed occur.

There are actually two morals to this story. The first is that God doesn't lie. If he promises to provide for our needs, he will. The second is that we must trust him and be willing to step out in faith. If Abram had refused to obey, it wouldn't have been God's fault that the promises were not fulfilled. Jesus promised that your Father in heaven will meet all of your needs (see Matthew 6:32–33). Do you believe him? Do something today to prove it.

Father, just like Abram, I choose to trust you,
step out in faith, and obey your will. No more
hanging back in fear and doubt for me—I know
you will provide for my needs in amazing ways.

NOVEMBER 21

"For with God nothing will be impossible." (Luke 1:37)

I am very thankful that the angel Gabriel spoke these words to the Blessed Mother and that they are recorded in the Bible. These words, the last spoken to Mary before she gave her consent to become the mother of the Savior, are among the most powerful in all of Scripture. Every time I face a difficult situation in life, I think of Gabriel's proclamation, and I am reminded of God's omnipotence.

While I can't say for certain, I believe I need to hear these words more than Mary did. Every day I encounter some challenge that requires me to place my trust in God's power. Some days I do better than others. If I really believed this statement, I would never let myself become overwhelmed by a problem that seems unfixable.

What situations in your life seem impossible? When you are tempted to feel anxious or discouraged, remember Gabriel's words and take heart!

Even though I know you can do all things,
God, I need to be reminded. Thank you for
including this powerful message in the Bible.

NOVEMBER 22

How long, O Lord? Will you forget
me for ever? (Psalm 13:1)

Do you have the courage to say this to God? Before you dismiss the psalmist's plea as being disrespectful, I invite you to look at it more closely. This is not a comment from someone who doesn't believe in the power of God. Rather it is a cry for help from a person who absolutely believes in God's ability to come to his assistance. If you're struggling with feelings that God has abandoned you, don't keep it to yourself. Let him know!

In the past I have been afraid of bothering God. My feeling was that he would get annoyed if I kept pestering him about the same thing. Since I have gotten to know him better, however, I understand that he wants me to keep asking him for what I need. There are numerous biblical examples that illustrate the value of persistent prayer. I can assure you that God hears all of your prayers. He will never forget you, but don't take my word for it. Cry out to him today. He won't be offended.

I have been waiting for you to answer me for so long, God!
I will continue to persevere in prayer, trusting that you will
give me patience and a new perspective on your timing.

NOVEMBER 23

After this many of his disciples drew back and no longer walked with him. (John 6:66)

The idea of consuming the Body and Blood of Jesus proved to be a challenge for some of his disciples. Exclaiming that it was a "hard saying" (see John 6:60), many of them walked away and stopped following him. And Jesus, making no attempt to water down the message or state that he was speaking figuratively, let them go. Like it or not, the truth is the truth. Jesus will not attempt to alter the truth in order to retain disciples.

If you have doubts about anything—from Church teachings to current situations in your life—don't make the mistake of imitating the disciples who walked away from Christ. Ask questions, do some research, and pray for a greater understanding. Jesus founded his Church to provide the answers we need.

Jesus, at times it is difficult for me to understand your Church's teachings, but I will not abandon you. I will continue to trust you while I seek answers to my questions.

NOVEMBER 24

"And so observe, from generation to generation, that none who put their trust in him will lack strength." (1 Maccabees 2:61)

Just before dying at the age of 146, Mattathias offered some great words to his sons. That advice has proven to be true throughout history. Anyone who trusts God possesses the strength to deal with anything. It worked in the past, and it will work today. The challenge is to put that trust into practice.

We put our trust in many things—wealth, other people, political analysts, meteorologists—but we have trouble trusting in God. Yet since the beginning of time, he has never abandoned his people or failed to deliver on his promises. Why do we have a hard time believing that he will give us the strength we need? If you put your trust in God, you will never be disappointed.

God, trusting you makes me strong—strong enough
to stop worrying and face life with courage and joy.

NOVEMBER 25

Then the Lord said, "I have seen the affliction of my people who are in Egypt, and have heard their cry because of their taskmasters." (Exodus 3:7)

One of the most painful feelings we can experience results from the belief that no one cares. No matter what kind of crisis we are facing, the burden is much lighter when we can share it with someone who is aware of what we're going through and willing to listen. As we can see by his words to Moses, God heard the cries of his people and was getting ready to assist them. He will do the same for you.

Even though this occurred several thousand years ago, the message remains the same. If you cry out to God, he will answer. His response might not come as quickly as you would like or in the manner you expect, but he will answer. God loves you and wants to fill you with his peace. If you are suffering, call out to him today.

Father, just as you came to the aid of the Israelites,
I know you will also assist me. Just knowing that
you care gives me courage and fills me with peace.

NOVEMBER 26

But understand this, that in the last days there
will come times of stress. (2 Timothy 3:1)

When I was twelve years old, my parents took me to the orthodontist for a consultation. He informed me that he would put braces on my teeth, and it would be painful at times. He was right. As much as I didn't want to hear it, it helped me to prepare for what was ahead. In some ways this knowledge made the pain easier to bear.

St. Paul delivers a similar message in this verse. Are we living in the last days? Absolutely. While we don't know when the world will end, we are in the period of time between the first and the second coming of Christ. Therefore we are in the last days. Just like my orthodontist, Paul tells it like it is, with no sugarcoating. He lets us know that during this time, we will encounter periods of stress.

Even when stressful events occur, however, you have the promise of spiritual strength to see you through. With Jesus in your life, you can be at peace no matter what happens.

Thank you for being honest with me, Jesus. With you by
my side, I can handle any times of stress in this world.

NOVEMBER 27

See what love the Father has given us,
that we should be called children of
God; and so we are. (1 John 3:1)

It's great to be loved, especially by God. Thinking about the
fact that he loves you unconditionally should make you feel
very special. As wonderful as that seems, however, there's
even more. He loves you so much that he has adopted you
as one of his children. Try thinking about that for a while!

When I was young I felt safe when my father was around.
I knew he loved me and would protect me from harm. Your
heavenly Father wants to serve that role in your life today.
Allow yourself to be childlike and learn to trust him. Whenever you are frightened, don't be afraid to cry out to him and
run into his open arms. It is there that you will find the peace
and security that you desire.

Heavenly Father, I'm so grateful to be your child.
Thank you for protecting me and keeping me safe.

NOVEMBER 28

"Fear not, therefore; you are of more value than many sparrows." (Matthew 10:31)

If you possess something of great value, you probably treat it with care. For example, it's highly unlikely that you would wear expensive clothing and jewelry while you were gardening. As a parent I would never intentionally allow my precious children to be placed in harmful situations. We always make it a point to guard our valuables.

Jesus wants us to understand just how valuable we are in the eyes of our heavenly Father. We mean so much to him, in fact, that he even knows the number of hairs on our heads. There is no area of your life that God considers unimportant. Let that thought bring you comfort as you deal with the "trivial" matters of life. He cares about you deeply. Share your concerns with him.

Father, I am sometimes hesitant to ask you for help with the trivial matters in my life. But if you know even the number of hairs on my head, no detail is too small for me to bring to you. What a relief!

NOVEMBER 29

"For as the heavens are higher than the earth, so are my ways higher than your ways and my thoughts than your thoughts." (Isaiah 55:9)

If I had to choose a go-to Bible verse, this one would be near the top of my list. I constantly need to be reminded that God is smarter than I am. He also thinks differently than we do. That's why we could never figure out why he does what he does. When his plan doesn't make sense to us, we should remember that God's ways are not our ways. He has the full picture—and on this side of heaven, we don't.

God is infinitely wiser than we are. As a result he sometimes chooses to do things that seem illogical to our limited human intelligence, causing us to miss the brilliance of his actions. Keep this verse in mind the next time you are faced with an inexplicable situation. God really does know what he's doing, even if it doesn't seem like it.

God, help me to trust you even when I can't understand your actions. I pray for wisdom and a greater understanding of your plans and purposes.

NOVEMBER 30

He is your praise; he is your God, who has done
for you these great and terrible things which
your eyes have seen. (Deuteronomy 10:21)

Take a moment to reflect on all the amazing things God has
done in your life. You were created out of nothing, your life is
being sustained by his mercy, and you have been redeemed.
If you add all of the unique blessings that you have been
given through the years, I'm sure your list will be quite long.

One of the best ways to overcome worrying about the
future is to recognize God's providence in the past. Sadly
we often neglect to take the time to do this. God has done
many great things for each of us. Getting into the habit of
reflecting on his goodness is a great way to stop worrying
about the road ahead.

*You have done many great things in my
life, God. As I reflect on them, I realize just
how much I have to be thankful for.*

DECEMBER 1

For God so loved the world that he gave his only-begotten Son, that whoever believes in him should not perish but have eternal life. (John 3:16)

I bet you've heard this verse before. It is so popular that it's almost impossible to avoid hearing it. Signs that proclaim "John 3:16" can even be seen at sporting events and concerts. While it can be argued that this is a good thing, there is also a downside that goes along with the familiarity of this Bible verse. It is so well-known that we can become desensitized to the power of its message.

Anyone who doubts God's love should become acquainted with this verse in a hurry. The Father's love is so great that he sent his Son to suffer and die so that we could be redeemed. Furthermore, sincerely following Jesus will result in eternal life. The amount of good news packed into that one sentence is astonishing. As we enter the Advent season, let this message fill your heart with hope.

Thank you for loving me so much that you sent your Son to redeem me, Father.

DECEMBER 2

I will give thanks to the Lord with my whole heart;
I will tell of all your wonderful deeds. (Psalm 9:1)

Giving thanks to the Lord is a great practice. It not only gets our minds off of our problems, it helps us to become grateful. But counting our blessings generally produces another result, one that can benefit many people: The more we realize what God has done for us, the more we want to share the news with others.

Are you in the habit of talking about your faith with those around you? Many people feel uncomfortable doing this, but I have discovered that the secret to overcoming this fear is getting to know Jesus. As your friendship with him grows, you will not be able to remain quiet about the blessings in your life. As you experience greater peace and joy, you won't be able to keep silent and will want to share him with everyone you know!

You have blessed me in so many ways, Jesus. Give
me opportunities to speak about you to those
around me, especially those who are struggling
with discouragement or full of anxiety.

DECEMBER 3

And there appeared to him an angel from heaven, strengthening him. (Luke 22:43)

On the night before he died, Jesus prayed to his Father using words that are both chilling and instructional: "Father, if you are willing, remove this chalice from me; nevertheless, not my will, but yours, be done" (see Luke 22:42). While Jesus' words teach us that it's certainly acceptable to ask for our suffering to end, it is crucial that we are willing to submit to the Father's will.

We never know for sure how God will answer our prayers. He may remove whatever is causing our suffering, or he may give us the grace to deal with it. Look at what happened with Jesus in the Garden of Gethsemane. He prayed for his suffering to end, and he received an angel to strengthen him. This enabled him to "pray more earnestly" (see Luke 22:44). Let the example of Jesus inspire you to bring all of your needs to prayer. Rest assured that your heavenly Father will give you exactly what you need.

God, I ask above all that your will be done in my life. I know that your grace is sufficient for me to make it through anything.

DECEMBER 4

So David prevailed over the Philistine with
a sling and with a stone, and struck the
Philistine, and killed him; there was no sword
in the hand of David. (1 Samuel 17:50)

The odds didn't appear to be in David's favor as he prepared to do battle with Goliath. Rejecting King Saul's attempt to suit him with armor, a helmet, and a spear, David chose to go into battle with a sling and five stones. But he also had some assistance that couldn't be seen with the naked eye, which would ultimately allow the brave warrior to emerge victorious over the menacing Philistine: He had God on his side.

No matter what challenge you face in life, having God's help is a game changer. With him on your side, you always have an advantage. You may not feel powerful, but you can do great things with God's help. Don't allow yourself to become discouraged. Just because the odds seem stacked against you, it doesn't mean you will be defeated. David was living proof of that!

*God, help me to remember that nothing is
impossible for me as long as you are by my side.
Today I will trust you with the giants in my life!*

DECEMBER 5

And the Word became flesh and
dwelt among us. (John 1:14)

The idea of God becoming man is one that most of us are comfortable with, mainly because it happened two thousand years ago. We know who Jesus is and what he did. We accept that this event happened, and we may even appreciate it from time to time. But this occurrence is such a radical example of God's love for us that it bears thinking about every day.

We can help the homeless without becoming homeless. We can help abused animals without living in a cage with them. We can support missionaries without traveling to a foreign country. God, on the other hand, loves us so much that he wanted to share our nature. While retaining his divinity, he became man. No matter what you face today, thinking about this should lighten your burden.

Jesus, thank you for loving me so much that you were willing to become man for my sake. Help me to remember that you understand what it means to be human and live on this earth.

DECEMBER 6

Then Amos answered Amaziah, "I am no prophet, nor a prophet's son; but I am a herdsman, and a dresser of sycamore trees." (Amos 7:14)

Do you ever feel that you're not qualified to share your faith with others? You want to draw others closer to Christ, but you don't feel you have what it takes. This is a common dilemma, one that most of us have experienced at one time or another.

Amos didn't view himself as a prophet, but God did. He asked the "herdsman" and "dresser of sycamore trees" to deliver an important message to the people. Amos wasn't chosen because he had an advanced theology degree. He was chosen because God decided he was the man for the job.

Millions of people in the world don't know that Jesus Christ is the source of all happiness. Some of those individuals are your coworkers and family members. Don't be afraid to tell them about Jesus. If you can't answer their questions, tell them you'll get back to them after you look up the answers. People need to hear what you have to say. Just like Amos, you *are* qualified.

Jesus, show me who needs to hear a word of encouragement today, or who is longing for someone to point the way to you. Grant me the courage to share your love with those around me.

DECEMBER 7

There is great gain in godliness with contentment; for we brought nothing into the world, and we cannot take anything out of the world; but if we have food and clothing, with these we shall be content. (1 Timothy 6:6–8)

Worrying about financial matters has become an epidemic in today's society. Even those who are financially stable can become anxious and worried that something *might* happen in the future to put them in financial jeopardy. As a result we hoard what we have and look for ways to increase our bank account balance. As our savings increase we feel secure, but this desire for more can become insatiable. How much is enough?

Learning to be content with what we have will bring us much peace. If we could put St. Paul's words to Timothy into practice every day, many of our anxieties would fade away. I suggest that you spend some time reading and rereading this verse throughout the day and see what happens. Are concerns about finances a source of anxiety and unrest for you? Are your needs being met? You may be surprised what you discover.

Jesus, I confess that my worrying is a sign of discontent and shows a lack of trust in you. Teach me to be content with what I have!

DECEMBER 8

Then he said to the disciple, "Behold your mother!" And from that hour the disciple took her to his own home. (John 19:27)

As he was dying on the cross, Jesus turned to his mother and "the disciple whom he loved" (traditionally believed to be St. John) and spoke four words that would change the world: "Woman, behold your son!" (John 19:26). It has always been the opinion of the Church that the beloved disciple represents all Christians. As a result we have been given the gift of Mary as our heavenly Mother.

By taking her into his home from that hour, John accepted Jesus' gift. How about you? Have you accepted the gift of Mary as your heavenly mother? For many years I ignored the words of our dying Savior, and it was one of the biggest mistakes I ever made. Accepting Mary as my mother has changed my life. As we celebrate the solemnity of Our Lady's Immaculate Conception today, now would be the perfect opportunity for you to take her into your own home. Just like any good mother, she wants what is best for you; you can count on her to lead you to Jesus and eternal life!

Mary, on this special day, I turn to you and accept you as my heavenly mother. Please pray for me!

DECEMBER 9

Count it all joy, my brethren, when you meet various trials, for you know that the testing of your faith produces steadfastness. (James 1:2–3)

Several years ago, when I was struggling with some challenges related to my full-time ministry, I reached out to a friend and asked for prayer. After assuring me that he would be praying, he pointed me to this Bible passage. And while I didn't realize it at the time, his suggestion was an excellent one. The words of St. James are a powerful reminder that the trials we encounter in life will help us to grow in faith.

Do you pray more often when your life is problem-free? My guess is that the answer is no. God understands that we have a tendency to forget him, and he often sends us various challenges to get our attention. Instead of looking at your problems in a negative light, look at them as a chance to grow closer to Christ. We tend to make the best spiritual progress during times of adversity. When the future is uncertain and all you see is darkness, you have something you don't have during times of tranquility: the opportunity to trust in Jesus.

God, thank you for giving me so many opportunities to trust you! I know that any difficulties I face will strengthen my character and help me grow closer to you.

DECEMBER 10

For we know that if the earthly tent we live
in is destroyed, we have a building from
God, a house not made with hands, eternal
in the heavens. (2 Corinthians 5:1)

Not too long ago I watched a news story about a tornado that devastated a small town. What I remember the most, however, is listening to a woman being interviewed after her home was completely destroyed. Even though she acknowledged the loss of her house, she was filled with gratitude and credited God with sparing the lives of her family. It was a powerful statement and showed great insight.

Look around you for a minute. Everything you see is temporary. All your possessions will remain behind when you move on to the next life. How would you react if a tornado or fire destroyed your house and you lost everything? Would you be able to thank God for his continued presence in your life, or would you be distraught over the loss of your possessions? The answer may be eye-opening.

God, teach me to appreciate your presence in my life.
You are greater than any possession I could ever have.

DECEMBER 11

[Jesus] said to him, "Follow me."
(John 21:19)

Jesus concluded his message to St. Peter with an invitation: "Follow me." Since these words were spoken shortly before Jesus ascended into heaven, they seem a bit out of place. Wasn't Peter already a follower of Jesus? Like many of us, he was being invited to take his discipleship to the next level.

If I truly desire to follow Jesus, I must give up my life. While this doesn't mean that I must become a martyr, it does mean that Christ must come first in my life. I must put myself at his disposal and let him use me in any way he sees fit. Although it sounds challenging, doing this will result in great peace. As he grew in faith, St. Peter reached a point where he was willing to give up his life and follow Jesus even more closely. How about you?

Jesus, I sense that you are inviting me to follow you more closely. Show me how I can take my relationship with you to a deeper level. When I lose courage and begin to doubt, please strengthen me and grant me peace.

DECEMBER 12

"And do not fear those who can kill the body but cannot kill the soul; rather fear him who can destroy both soul and body in hell." (Matthew 10:28)

Chances are that even if you are not a chronic worrier, there is something that frightens you. Finances, the unknown, health problems, religious persecution, natural disasters, public speaking, and numerous other situations can make you afraid at times. But in the entire Bible, amid countless "Be not afraid" messages, God only tells us to fear one thing. Sadly it's something that very few people fear in this day and age: the very real possibility of spending eternity in hell.

Even though this book is designed to help you overcome anxiety, I am not going to sugarcoat Jesus' message. The devil is real, he's out to destroy you, and he wants you to spend eternity in hell. He will lie to you, play on your fears, entice you with temptation, and do anything in his power to convince you to turn away from God. The good news is that the devil does not have the power to make you do anything, and God gives you the grace to resist all of his tricks. Pay attention and take the threats of the evil one seriously, but trust in God and you will be victorious.

God, please protect me from the threat of the evil one today.

DECEMBER 13

Your eyes beheld my unformed substance; in
your book were written, every one of them,
the days that were formed for me, when as yet
there were none of them. (Psalm 139:16)

Does the idea of an unknown future frighten you? Well, here's some news that should make you feel better. Your future may be unknown to you, but it's not unknown to God. As this verse proclaims, every one of your days was planned before you even existed.

As you face each new day, remember that God is always in control. Nothing that happens to you surprises him. He has a plan for your life, and it is guaranteed to bring you joy if you trust him.

One day when I was flying to a speaking engagement, the pilot made an interesting announcement as we were about to take off. It's a message that could easily be spoken to us by God each day: "My job is to get you to your destination safely. Your job is to enjoy the ride."

God, nothing that happens to me will ever
surprise you. Teach me to stop worrying,
trust you, and enjoy the journey.

DECEMBER 14

*Now may the Lord of peace himself
give you peace at all times in all
ways. (2 Thessalonians 3:16)*

As he prepares to close his second letter to the Thessalonians, St. Paul offers a very special prayer for the people. He prays that they may have God's peace at all times in all ways. Note that he isn't just praying for peace during good times, but at *all* times. This implies that it is possible to experience peace even during times of difficulty. Isn't that a reassuring thought?

Taking a page out of St. Paul's book, I am praying for you as I write this. I pray that God will bless you with his supernatural peace at all times. May he bless and keep you all of the days of your life, and may you find comfort in good times and bad.

*Thank you for the gift of your peace today, Jesus.
Please bless those I love with peace, too.*

DECEMBER 15

And the angel said to her, "Do not be afraid, Mary, for you have found favor with God." (Luke 1:30)

When we think of the Blessed Mother, we generally don't picture her afraid, but the words of the angel paint a different picture. By reflecting on Gabriel's message, we are reminded of the fact that Mary was human. She experienced the emotion of fear, just as we do.

Mary's life demonstrates that it is totally possible to be afraid and follow God's will at the same time. We sometimes mistakenly think we're committing a sin just because we are experiencing normal human emotions. The real truth is liberating: If you are afraid of something God is asking you to do but you do it anyway, you are following his will perfectly. As you grow closer to God, your fear will gradually decrease. For now, however, just relax. Remember that Mary was afraid at times, too!

God, I will continue to obey you even when I am afraid.
I'm grateful that obedience is a great cure for worry!

DECEMBER 16

Stretch forth your hand to the poor, so that your blessing may be complete. (Sirach 7:32)

Reaching out to the poor is not something that typically comes to mind when trying to overcome anxiety, but it is a critical step, for many reasons. For one thing, Jesus wants us to encounter him in the poor. Therefore, if you want to know him (and experience his peace), look around and do something to help those who are destitute.

It might seem difficult to see Jesus when we come face-to-face with people who are down and out, but he stressed that anything we do for the poor, we do for him (see Matthew 25:31–46). We can get so wrapped up in our own daily struggles that we lose sight of this important teaching. No matter how many problems you are facing, always make it a point to do at least one kind act for someone in need each day. That person might be physically needy or spiritually destitute, but remember that with this kind act, you are showing kindness to Jesus himself.

*Thank you for the gift of the poor, Jesus. I know
that whatever I do for them, I do for you.*

DECEMBER 17

"I am the Alpha and the Omega, the beginning and the end. To the thirsty I will give water without price from the fountain of the water of life." (Revelation 21:6)

Chances are good that you have one or more pressing needs in your life right now. While the needs may vary (financial issues, health problems, loneliness, addiction, career ambitions), I bet that you associate the fulfillment of these needs with greater happiness. Am I correct? Let me share with you a lesson that has taken me more than fifty years to learn: You will never be truly happy without having a close, personal relationship with Jesus Christ.

The best news of all is that there is no monetary cost for the peace Jesus wants to give you. There is a cost, however. In order to experience Christian joy, you must learn to put God first in your life. He comes first, and everything else comes second. Choose to make time for him every day. Tell him your concerns, express your love for him, ask for his wisdom, and thank him for your blessings. Doing this on a regular basis will bring lasting peace.

Jesus, I realize that you are the source of all happiness. Thank you for the joy and peace you so abundantly give me.

DECEMBER 18

"As for you, you meant evil against me; but God meant it for good, to bring it about that many people should be kept alive, as they are today." (Genesis 50:20)

Joseph had every reason to be angry with his brothers after they sold him into slavery. In his wisdom, however, he understood that there was a bigger picture and recognized that their actions were part of God's plan to save the lives of many people. Showing great compassion, he forgave their evil betrayal and shared this message with them.

When I was laid off in 2012, I experienced mixed feelings. Although I had been unhappy with my job, I felt betrayed by those who decided that I should be let go. Eventually, though, I realized that this was part of God's plan to steer me into a new career as a speaker and author. Seeing the big picture allowed me to experience peace and to forgive those involved in the decision-making process. Everything that happens in our lives is orchestrated by God and part of his plan. Accepting that will always bring us peace.

God, help me to accept that everything that happens in my life comes from you.

DECEMBER 19

The light shines in the darkness, and the darkness has not overcome it. (John 1:5)

When you turn on the light in a dark room, the darkness vanishes and the room is filled with light. As uncomfortable as it feels to be in a dark room, however, it's much more threatening to be living in a dark world. Fortunately the presence of Jesus Christ overcomes the darkness we face each day.

You may not realize it, but you have a great deal of control over how much light will shine in your life. If you choose to immerse yourself in reality shows, tabloids, and even the nightly news, your mind will be filled with darkness. If, on the other hand, you make faith a regular part of your day, you will be filled with light.

In the past a constant diet of sports talk radio, self-indulgence, and instant gratification made my life miserable. It wasn't until I met Jesus personally and began following him that things turned around for me. Always remember, Jesus Christ is the light of the world. No amount of darkness will ever change that.

Jesus, thank you for being my light in the darkness. I choose to walk in your light and allow it to shine brightly in my life.

DECEMBER 20

Then the Lord said to Moses, "Behold, I will
rain bread from heaven for you; and the people
shall go out and gather a day's portion every
day, that I may test them." (Exodus 16:4)

This might date me, but I remember the days when many professional baseball players had winter jobs. Long-term, multimillion-dollar contracts put an end to that practice and, as many will argue, took away the incentive to produce on the playing field. As humans we have a tendency to work harder if there is a reward involved.

God understands this weakness and wants to help us. Walking by faith requires trust. If God had given the Israelites enough food to last for several months, I'm pretty sure they would have forgotten him until they needed more. As much as you wish that all your problems and challenges would miraculously disappear, they exist to serve as a reminder that you need God in your life. Make it a point to start each day by asking for the grace to sustain you in the midst of them.

God, thank you for supplying me with exactly the right
amount of grace that I require to live this day well.

DECEMBER 21

May the God of peace himself sanctify you
wholly; and may your spirit and soul and body
be kept sound and blameless at the coming of
our Lord Jesus Christ. (1 Thessalonians 5:23)

Who among us isn't looking for peace? The fact that you are reading this book is a good indication that peace is a priority for you, as it should be. The quest for peace is especially beneficial when it leads us to the God of peace himself.

The world is filled with people searching for peace. Many of them do not realize, however, that their desire can only be fulfilled by Jesus Christ. As a result of their misunderstanding, they seek peace in material things and empty pleasures, which can never fulfill them. Those of us who have been there realize that true peace can only exist if we have a relationship with Jesus. Somebody in your life needs to hear this today.

*Jesus, show me someone who is longing for
peace but looking in the wrong places.*

DECEMBER 22

And suddenly there was a great earthquake, so
that the foundation of the prison was shaken;
and immediately all the doors were opened and
everyone's chains were unfastened. (Acts 16:26)

Do you believe in miracles? After watching the events detailed in this verse, the jailer guarding Paul and Silas certainly did. Shortly after the earthquake, he was baptized, along with all the members of his family. We don't know for certain if it was the display of God's power, the evangelization efforts of Paul and Silas, or a combination of both that converted the jailer, but we do know the end result. All in all, this was an amazing chain of events that drew a lost soul and his family to God.

While there are many possible messages we might extract from this verse, here is an important takeaway: If you have a problem in your life, ask God to handle it. If he wants it fixed, it will happen—even if he has to create an earthquake that causes cell doors to be opened and chains to be unfastened!

God, I believe that you still perform miracles
today. I will trust you to do the impossible in
the tough situations I am facing right now.

DECEMBER 23

For to us a child is born, to us a son is given; and the government will be upon his shoulder, and his name will be called "Wonderful Counselor, Mighty God, Everlasting Father, Prince of Peace." (Isaiah 9:6)

In a few days we will celebrate the birth of our Savior. As this prophesy from Isaiah reveals, the arrival of the Messiah was not a spur-of-the-moment decision. Whether we realize it or not, God always has a plan. Furthermore, that plan is always perfect.

What is the greatest need in your life? While the answer may differ from person to person, there is one need that we all have in common: the need for a Savior. This need has already been met because Jesus was willing to come to earth and die for our sins. If your greatest need has already been met, what makes you think that God won't take care of everything else?

Thank you for meeting my greatest need, Father.
I know that you will always keep your promises
with everything else that concerns me!

DECEMBER 24

Your words were found, and I ate them, and your words became to me a joy and the delight of my heart. (Jeremiah 15:16)

Are you tired of feeling stressed out day after day? I'll share a secret with you. After years of experiencing daily anxiety, I have discovered an activity that brings me incredible peace. I know it can have the same effect in your life. The secret is to read the Bible every day.

As you develop the habit of reading Scripture daily, you will begin to experience the peace God wants you to have. If you think you're too busy to read the Bible or that you won't understand it, you will be closing off one of God's favorite means of communication. It may seem difficult at first, but it gets better with time. Before reading, ask the Holy Spirit to guide you. If you want to enhance the experience, try reading your Bible in the presence of the Blessed Sacrament. I am confident you will soon understand what Jeremiah meant when he wrote this verse.

Jesus, I will set aside a little time every day to read my Bible. Please open my mind to hear your voice. Thank you for providing this source of spiritual nourishment for me!

DECEMBER 25

And she gave birth to her first-born son and wrapped him in swaddling cloths, and laid him in a manger, because there was no place for him in the inn. (Luke 2:7)

This verse makes it real, doesn't it? Two thousand years ago our Savior was born in Bethlehem. He came into this world to redeem you. Not only did Jesus experience the lack of comfort that goes along with being human, but he was criticized, rejected, tortured, and ultimately put to death. He willingly did this out of love for you.

Spend some time reflecting on this today. Tell Jesus you want to welcome him more deeply into your heart. Thank him for his willingness to suffer for you, and tell him how much you love him. Ask him to walk with you and help you with your daily struggles. You'll find out why he is called the Prince of Peace!

Thank you for becoming man for my sake, Lord. You are the best friend I could ever have! Show me how I can welcome you more fully into my heart.

DECEMBER 26

What have you that you did not receive? If then you received it, why do you boast as if it were not a gift? (1 Corinthians 4:7)

When we're overcome by problems, it can be difficult to count our blessings. I have been there many times in my life, and my natural tendency is to feel sorry for myself and wallow in my misery. Although it takes effort, we can and should overcome this tendency. No matter how I feel, I force myself to thank God for my blessings every day.

Overcoming anxiety often involves changing the way we think. We may not be able to control many of the events around us, but we can control our thoughts. If you start each day by listing your blessings, you will feel more positive than if you choose to obsess over your problems.

Don't take my word for it, however. Try it out for yourself. Every morning thank God for giving you another day, and then proceed to list (and thank him for) all the things you are grateful for. This simple practice has totally changed my outlook on life; it can change yours, too.

Thank you for all the blessings in my life, God. As I go through my day today, I will continue to focus on your goodness toward me instead of dwelling on my problems.

DECEMBER 27

For unclean spirits came out of many who were possessed, crying with a loud voice; and many who were paralyzed or lame were healed. (Acts 8:7)

Contrary to popular belief, Jesus didn't stop performing miracles when he ascended into heaven. Even though he no longer walked the earth, Christ continued to do miraculous things. Only now he worked through people like the apostles.

If you feel discouraged today, there is a very good chance that you have forgotten about God's power to work miracles in your life and the lives of those around you. Let this verse serve as documented proof of his ability to work in your life. The only thing that has changed is that Jesus no longer has an earthly body of flesh and bones.

Jesus, thank you for still being a God of miracles! Take away my discouragement and fill me with the faith that you can do great things in my life.

DECEMBER 28

Riches do not profit in the day of wrath, but righteousness delivers from death. (Proverbs 11:4)

It's been said many times that money doesn't buy happiness. As this verse indicates, it doesn't get us into heaven either. If both of these statements are true, why do so many individuals make wealth their ultimate goal in life?

The love of comfort is a major obstacle in the pursuit of holiness. We don't like to be uncomfortable and will often try to do anything to avoid it. But God loves you too much to give you happiness merely in this world. He wants you to be happy not just for a few years, but forever. Placing your trust in him, not in money or the comfort it can buy, is the only way to achieve eternal joy.

Sometimes I get distracted by my desire to be comfortable, Jesus. Help me to remember that I was created to live with you in heaven. I want to stop worrying about my comfort level and experience true happiness!

DECEMBER 29

What is man that you are mindful of him, and the son of man that you care for him? (Psalm 8:4)

If you want to feel loved and blessed, then ponder this question. As important as it is to reflect on the question, it's even more important to think about the answer. There is nothing that you can ever do to earn God's love. Furthermore, there is nothing that you can ever do to make him stop loving you. He loves you . . . period!

It's amazing to be loved unconditionally. No matter how much I am loved by any human, nothing compares to the love of my Father in heaven. The more I think about his love, the more grateful I am . . . and the more I love him in return.

Heavenly Father, I don't know why you love me,
but I'm so grateful that you do. I love you, too!

DECEMBER 30

But Jesus looked at them and said to them,
"With men this is impossible, but with God
all things are possible." (Matthew 19:26)

How many times have you thought (or even said) that something is impossible? It may involve a sports team making it into the playoffs, a loved one returning to the Church, or a friend being cured of cancer. As Jesus reminds us in this verse, however, nothing is impossible for God.

This is one of those verses that are permanently etched in my memory; I refer to it often. And whenever I think about these words, I am filled with hope. Jesus didn't make any exceptions. Being healed of cancer, freedom from loneliness, recovery from addiction, overcoming anxiety, getting to heaven—it's all possible. Before you decide that something is impossible, think about what Jesus said. You just might want to reconsider.

I know that all things are possible for you,
God. Thank you for giving me hope in the
midst of my own "impossible" challenges.

DECEMBER 31

"You also must be ready; for the Son of man is coming at an hour you do not expect." (Luke 12:40)

As the year comes to a close, it's a good idea to reflect on the fact that our lives will also come to an end. Immediately after dying we will be judged by God. While we don't want to become obsessed with the idea of judgment, the fact that we are accountable for our actions should motivate us to live our lives in a holy manner.

God doesn't expect you to become holy by yourself. Instead he expects you to ask for the grace that you need each day. If you want to stop worrying, break a bad habit, or get to know him better, Jesus is available to help you. Never be afraid to take him up on his offer.

Tomorrow we enter into a new year. Look at it as a new beginning, a fresh start. With God by your side, you can confidently face the future with all its blessings and challenges.

God, I realize that I am responsible for all of my thoughts, words, and actions. As I get ready to start a new year, show me how to live my life in a manner pleasing to you. With the help of your grace, I know this is possible. I'm grateful for all I've learned this year, and I look forward to the future!

May the God of hope fill you with

all joy and peace in believing,

so that by the power of the Holy

Spirit you may abound in hope.

ROMANS 15:13

GARY ZIMAK is the author of several books, including *From Fear to Faith* and *Faith, Hope, and Clarity.* He is a frequent speaker at parishes and conferences across the United States and Canada, has an international radio following, and is recognized as the leading Catholic speaker on the topic of overcoming anxiety. In addition to hosting his own daily radio show on BlogTalkRadio, Gary is a regular guest on EWTN television and radio. Gary resides in New Jersey with his wife, Eileen, and twin daughters, Mary and Elizabeth.